THE FUNDRAISING SERIES

CAPITAL
CAMPAIGNS

Trudy Hayden

DSC · Institute of Fundraising

Charities Aid Foundation

The fundraising series
Community Fundraising Harry Brown (editor)
Corporate Fundraising Valerie Morton (editor)
Fundraising Databases Peter Flory
Fundraising Strategy Redmond Mullin
Legacy Fundraising Sebastian Wilberforce (editor)
Trust Fundraising Anthony Clay (editor)
Marketing Strategy Peter Maple
Major Donor Fundraising Margaret Holman and Lucy Sargent (July 2006)
(See p vii for further information)

Copyright © 2006 Directory of Social Change

The moral right of the author has been asserted in accordance with
the Copyrights, Designs and Patents Act 1988.

Published by
The Director of Social Change   Tel 020 7209 5151
24 Stephenson Way   Fax 020 7391 4804
London   e-mail: publications@dsc.org.uk
NW1 2DP

Customer services Tel 08450 77 7707 from whom further copies and
a full publications list are available.

The Directory of Social Change is a Registered Charity no. 800517

Original text and cover design by Eugenie Dodd Typographics
Typeset by Keystroke, Jacaranda Lodge, Wolverhampton
Printed and bound by Page Bros, Norwich

British Library Cataloguing in Publication Data
A catalogue record for this book is available from the British Library

ISBN-10 1 903991 62 5
ISBN-13 978 1 903991 62 6

Contents

APPENDIX

The fundraising series

Fundraising is a profession in a constant state of evolution; to meet the challenge that this presents, fundraisers must also evolve. Fundraisers look to the future, anticipate need and develop new techniques to fulfil it. The CAF, Institute of Fundraising, DSC fundraising series seeks to address the full range of fundraising activity and technique in one series.

Each successive volume addresses one key element in the full battery of fundraising skills. As the series develops, it will cover the broadest spectrum of fundraising experience currently available. Like fundraising itself, there is no finate limit to the series. As fields develop, so new titles will be added and old ones revised.

The titles are intended not as manuals or directories but as texts explaining and debating fundraising within a framework that derives from the workplace. These texts are to be written as well as used by academics and practitioners alike. Each title addresses the core competencies within the Institute of Fundraising's Certificate of Fundraising Management, ensuring their relevance to working practice.

Each title aims to place the activity covered in the text within its historical, ethical and theoretical context, demonstrating its relationship to current practice. The main body of the text proceeds to analyse current activity and to identify the constituent areas needed to guide future strategy.

The Institute of Fundraising is well situated to assist in the production of this series; without the support, assistance and expertise of its members and their colleagues, the continued development of the series would not be possible. I would like to thank all those who have contributed and are currently contributing to what continues to be the most comprehensive fundraising sereis available today.

Andrew Watt
Head of policy, Institute of Fundraising

About the author

Trudy Hayden is a strategic planning and fundraising consultant in the US and UK. She retired in 2002 having worked as Senior Director of Foundation and Government Support at the American Museum of Natural History. She was previously Manager of Program Development and Foundation Relations and Deputy Director of the Campaign at The New York Public Library from 1984 to 1994, and Director of Foundation Relations at the Natural Resources Defense Council, an environmental advocacy organisation, from 1994 to 1997.

She ran two successful and highly visible campaigns at the The New York Public Library – the first of which established a model of campaign structure that has been widely imitated throughout the US and the UK.

Since her retirement Trudy has worked as a fundraising consultant in New York, including a capital campaign planning for a theatre company. For several years she has led training courses on capital campaign planning and management for the Directory of Social Change.

In her 'pre-fundraising life' she worked for many years as a policy analyst and advocate in the field of civil liberties and civil rights, including as Director of the American Civil Liberties Union's National Privacy Rights Project in the 1970s. She is a graduate of Swarthmore College and Columbia University.

Introduction

Fundraising appeals to build museums and cathedrals or to endow colleges and 'foundations for the relief of the poor' have been around for centuries. But it is only since the 1980s that charities and other voluntary organisations have developed the notion of a capital campaign as a precisely defined, tightly structured fundraising strategy. Over the years, the experiments and experiences of many different kinds of voluntary organisations have produced a set of principles and procedures for planning a successful capital campaign – principles and procedures that have been tested and found applicable to all kinds and sizes of organisations and all sorts of fundraising goals. If you are contemplating a capital campaign, you can increase your chances of success by understanding these principles and adapting them to your own circumstances.

It is not implied that you will fail unless you structure your capital campaign in a rigidly prescribed manner or follow the processes described in this book to the letter. But if you understand the logic behind these processes, you can make an informed decision to deviate from them for good reason, and perhaps invent an adaptation that more closely suits your needs. Even if you expect to employ a consultant to help design and manage your campaign, you need to be familiar with the principles of planning because, as you will see, they require the participation and commitment of everyone in the organisation. Capital campaign planning is not a responsibility that can be delegated.

This book is addressed to fundraisers, chief executives, and other management staff as well as trustees and members of management committees – anyone who will be involved in planning and running a capital campaign, or in the initial decision to undertake a capital campaign. It does not attempt to explain the basic skills and techniques of fundraising, assuming that many readers will themselves be experienced fundraisers. Those who are not may wish to consult the *Further Reading* section at the end of the book.

A word about the organisations and campaigns mentioned throughout this book. All are real, but are referred to by fictitious names. Using such a wide variety of examples helps to make the point that a systematic process of campaign planning is as valid for a small, relatively young community-based charity as it is for a large, well-established, structurally complex organisation. The process is based on a set of analytical exercises that allow you to define and sift through a wide range of options and to choose those that will best serve your mission, your needs, and your priorities at this moment in your organisation's history.

Capital campaigns are hard work, and they are risky. But a successful capital campaign will make you stronger, more creative, more effective, more visible, and more resilient. It is hoped that this book will help you plan a successful capital campaign.

CHAPTER ONE
What is a capital campaign?

In fundraising terminology, a capital campaign (or capital appeal) is defined as:

> a coordinated institutional effort, with a specified goal and timetable, to increase an organisation's permanent assets – a building, a significant expansion of programme, endowment, or a combination of these – that will lift the organisation to a higher level of performance.

This chapter describes the different types of capital campaigns, explores how a capital campaign differs from fundraising for ongoing operating revenue, and highlights some of the risks, as well as the unique opportunities, inherent in a capital campaign.

Varieties of capital campaigns

The most commonly understood meaning of the term 'capital campaign' is a fundraising effort to acquire or construct a building. This might include the purchase of a site, the design and construction of a new building, major expansion of an existing building (such as a new wing), or the complete reconfiguration and refurbishment of an existing facility. It normally does not, however, refer to more limited schemes for redecoration or refurnishing or the installation of new computer or telecommunications equipment unless these are integral to a larger construction project.

A second type of capital campaign launches a substantial programme initiative or the replication of an existing programme in another location. For example, an organisation that teaches dramatic arts might decide to expand its range by starting a music or dance division. Or, an organisation that offers services for children with learning disabilities might have the opportunity to recreate one of its most successful services in a nearby town or city. It may come as a surprise to some readers that this type of fundraising effort is considered a capital campaign. Remember, the distinctive characteristic of a capital campaign is the creation of significant new, permanent assets, such as in the examples just mentioned. The expansion of

1

an existing project by adding a few more staff or some new enhancements would not be regarded as a capital campaign.

The third type of capital campaign is intended to create endowment. Endowment is a fund in which the capital is held separately from the organisation's other assets and invested. A portion of the revenue from investment (usually equal to 4–6% of the worth of the capital fund) is drawn each year for ongoing operating support, with any additional earnings ploughed back into the capital fund so that the fund grows over time to keep up with increasing costs. The benefit of endowment is that it provides a steady, dependable stream of revenue year after year, which helps to relieve the pressure of fundraising for operating support. However, there is a sense in which fundraising for endowment is a costly expenditure of effort. You can raise £500,000 for current operating revenue to be used immediately, or you can raise £500,000 for endowment, which, with a draw at 5%, will produce only £25,000 for current operating revenue each year. Raising endowment is usually possible only for established organisations with substantial fundraising capacity, but it is extremely valuable because it helps to secure the organisation's future against the vagaries of the fundraising climate.

Most capital campaigns are in fact multi-purpose. A campaign to construct a new building might also encompass new programme initiatives that will be housed in the building. Endowment is often part of a building campaign, to assure the future upkeep of the facility and the activities that will take place within it. And crucially, capital campaigns incorporate important purposes that are not for the creation of new capital at all: ongoing operating support for current activities, enhancements to current activities, and the shift to a permanently higher level of operating revenue to support the organisation's expanding assets.

Why capital campaigns are not 'business as usual'

Let's look again at the definition of a capital campaign and focus on some important differences between capital campaigns and fundraising 'business as usual'.

• A capital campaign is, above all, a coordinated institutional effort. It is not a discrete task that can be delegated to your fundraising staff or development department; it requires commitment and participation from every part of the organisation (trustees, administration, staff, and volunteers) in a well-planned, synchronised set of activities in which everyone has a critical role to play. Ideally, of course, fundraising would always be structured as a coordinated organisational effort, but it often happens that a capital campaign becomes the catalyst for creating this integration.

• A capital campaign has a defined goal and timetable: a clear beginning and a clear end, with specified and publicly declared financial and programme targets. These targets must be met, or the campaign will be seen to fail.

• A capital campaign increases the organisation's permanent assets, that is, its total net worth. A capital campaign makes the organisation grow, quickly and dramatically.

• The purpose of a capital campaign is to lift the organisation to a higher level of performance. It is about change, increased effectiveness, and the achievement of a bold vision of the organisation's future.

Risks and opportunities

The very qualities that make a capital campaign different from everyday fundraising create both risks and opportunities. If you know in advance what they are, you can prepare to minimise the risks and grasp the opportunities.

Risks

• It is risky to undertake a capital campaign without first determining whether this is the right move at the right time for your organisation. There may be more urgent needs and issues that could threaten your well-being if they are neglected or shunted aside for a capital campaign.

• It is risky to undertake a capital campaign without having a full understanding of the organisational resources, skills, and effort involved. This does not mean just the financial resources, but also the human effort of trustees, staff, and volunteers that will be required.

• Some campaigns flounder because the organisation has not identified, in advance, specific sources of funding for all of its campaign goals. Reliance on 'something turning up' is a common, and dangerous, mistake. Experienced fundraisers know that gifts don't just 'turn up': we make them happen.

• Some campaigns flounder because the organisation underestimates the costs of creating new assets. Building projects, in particular, are notorious for exceeding their budgets and timetables. When this happens, you will end the campaign with a deficit, or you will have to scramble desperately to raise additional funds.

- Some campaigns fail even when they appear to succeed, because the organisation has not realistically estimated the costs of supporting its new assets and is ill-prepared to maintain a higher level of operating revenue into the indefinite future.

- Some campaigns cause enormous disruption because the focus on raising capital funds undercuts efforts to raise ongoing operating revenue for current activities.

- Even a campaign that meets its goals can be stressful because the very fact of running a capital campaign will stretch your energy and resources to their limits.

Having acknowledged that a capital campaign can be risky, it is just as important to understand that a capital campaign can open doors to new opportunities, unleash creativity, encourage bold thinking, and enhance your organisational capacity. Yes, you want to avoid the pitfalls, but you also want to exploit the campaign not merely as a device for raising money, but as a mechanism for positive growth and change.

Opportunities

- The visibility of a capital campaign will put your organisation into the public spotlight. It will introduce your work and accomplishments to new audiences, new stakeholders, and potential new donors.

- The stated objectives of your capital campaign will demonstrate your relevance, your vibrancy, and your skills and achievements to the wider community.

- A well-planned capital campaign can expand your circle of support – not just financial support (though that is crucial), but also community and public good will.

- The process of planning a capital campaign will enable you to define and pursue your highest priorities and most effective strategies.

- A capital campaign will develop and strengthen organisational skills.

- A capital campaign, if it is properly planned and executed, will increase the participation and commitment of your trustees, your volunteers, and your donors.

- Finally, remember the definition of the purpose of a capital campaign: to create new assets that lift the organisation to a higher level of performance. You will become not just bigger, but better.

The key to confronting both risk and opportunity is planning. That is what we will discuss in the succeeding chapters of this book: a thoughtful, systematic process for planning and managing a successful capital campaign.

CHAPTER TWO
Do you need a capital campaign?

'We've been playing for fifteen years in rented theatres. But they're never really right for our kind of experimental productions. It's time for us to have our own theatre, built to our specifications.'

So, it seems like a good idea to start planning a capital campaign, right? Not necessarily.

If you envisage a capital campaign that will enhance your organisation's capabilities and serve its mission, you must first identify the most compelling challenges and needs that confront you, and then determine the actions that will most effectively address them. Only then can you decide whether a capital campaign – and what kind of capital campaign – is right for you.

There is an established mechanism for exploring these issues: it is called strategic planning. A strategic plan is:

a systematic process through which an organisation commits itself to actions that advance the implementation of its mission and are responsive to the environment in which it operates.

A well-planned, well-managed capital campaign is built on the foundation of a strategic plan. In fact, not only can strategic planning tell you whether you need a capital campaign; it will also help define many of the elements that will be included in the campaign and shape the way you present your campaign to potential donors and the wider public. This chapter will take you through a simplified outline of strategic planning, and show you how the strategic plan can focus your fundraising efforts on high-priority, well-defined goals.

The key questions of strategic planning

Strategic planning addresses four key questions about your organisation:

- why?
- where?

- whither?
- how?

The process of answering these questions gives you the substance and the structure of your strategic plan.

Why?

The first step in a strategic plan is to write a statement of mission and values. Why does your organisation exist, and what are the changes you want to bring about in people's lives, in the community, in the world? In fundraising terminology, the answer to this query is called your 'mission'. What sets you apart from other organisations working on the same or similar issues? What are the shared organisational values that guide the pursuit of your mission? In fundraising terminology, the answers to these queries are called your 'values' or 'principles'.

The questions appear straightforward, but the responses are more subtle and complex than you might expect. You need to express your mission in a way that demonstrates to the outside world your unique organisational niche in a competitive marketplace. You also need to frame it in a way that will guide your own decision-making and keep you from taking paths that may seem attractive, but that could divert your focus from your core purpose.

You are writing a mission statement for internal strategic planning, not for public consumption (that comes later), so you want to keep your statement lean, avoid vague or emotive language, and make every word count. Your mission statement is not a laundry list of your activities, but a clear expression of your purpose (the end result you seek to accomplish) and the means you use to achieve your purpose.

Example 1:

HOME assists ex-prisoners in North London to re-enter the community by offering transitional housing, employment counselling and training, and referral to mental health, drug counselling, and other support services that will help them achieve stable, productive, fulfilling lives.

Example 2:

Save Our Wildlife seeks to prevent the loss of endangered and threatened wildlife and their habitats in West Yorkshire through public education and the creation of community-based wildlife conservation projects, in order to preserve these precious natural resources for future generations.

A bit dry, perhaps, but enough to tell us why these organisations exist and the general outline of their activities, including such critical information as whether they are local, regional, or national in scope.

But a mission statement alone does not give us the complete answer. We also need to know something about the values and principles that guide these organisations as they go about their business. HOME, for example, might operate on the principle that ex-prisoners are themselves best qualified to understand the needs of other ex-prisoners. Its statement of values would emphasise its respect for the dignity of ex-prisoners as equal, functioning members of the community and the leadership of ex-prisoners in the design and delivery of its services. Another organisation serving ex-prisoners might have a religious connection, and therefore all of its activities will be shaped by the tenets of that faith. Several organisations working in the same field may have sharply different 'profiles' because they operate in accordance with different values.

Crafting the answer to 'why' is probably the most important step in the strategic planning process. You will measure everything that follows against your mission and values statements, pursuing those activities that further your mission and values, eschewing those that do not.

The first segment of your strategic plan, therefore, will look like this:

Strategic Planning Worksheet 1: missions and values

MISSION

_____
_____
_____
_____
_____
_____
_____

VALUES

_____
_____
_____
_____
_____
_____

Where?

Where are you at this moment? What is the environment in which your organisation operates? What are the external and internal factors that will shape its future? What are your most compelling opportunities and challenges? What past accomplishments and current strengths can you identify as the foundation on which to build a successful future?

This is a fact-finding exercise. It requires that you assess both the external environment and the internal state of your organisation.

As you look at the external environment, ask what political, economic, social, or other factors are altering your audience, your clients, or your community. Are the demographics of your audiences or clients changing? Are their needs and expectations changing? What broader societal factors – economic trends, government policy, legal requirements – are likely to have an impact on your services, your financial stability, your staffing, or your ability to expand? Have other organisations appeared in your community or on the national scene whose services compete with yours, or whose services complement yours? What changes in the funding climate might affect your ability to raise money? For example, have some previously reliable governmental funding sources been discontinued, or conversely, is there an influx of new business in your community that might become a source of support for your work?

Now look internally. With honesty, assess your leadership and governance, your staffing structure and skills, your capacity for staff training and development, your ability to measure the effectiveness of your programmes, your financial stability and capacity for financial management, the clarity of your financial reporting, the state of your physical plant, the state of your technology and information systems, your communications and marketing abilities, the size and stability of your donor base, your capacity for generating earned revenue, and your administrative and management structures. Where might you need to adapt to meet changing circumstances?

Your initial inventory of the external and internal environments might look something like the worksheet shown on page 00. Note that the external and internal factors listed are only illustrative; you should include anything and everything that seems relevant. It doesn't matter how long the list is, because in the next planning segment you will sift through it to decide what is most important.

Next, from your assessment of the external and internal environments identify the key factors that will determine how you operate and grow in the future. What are your most compelling challenges and opportunities? For example, as a community family services centre perhaps you have noted a strong shift in the demographics of your client population toward an older age group and a substantial influx of Asian immigrants; changes in government regulations that will affect the way you provide services to

Strategic Planning Worksheet 2: external and internal assessment

External factors	
Client/community demographics	
Client needs/expectations	
Economic environment	
Government regulations/policy	
Legal requirements	
Changes in funding climate/new funding opportunities/loss of funding opportunities	
Competition from other organisations	
etc.	
Internal factors	
Leadership/governance	
Staff skills/structure/training	
Effectiveness of services	
Financial stability	
Clarity of financial reporting/ financial management	
Physical plant/equipment	
Size/stability of donor base	
Sources of earned revenue	
Administration/management	
etc.	

certain clients, such as those with specific types of mental health needs; the emergence of several new charities in your community whose activities appear to complement but not duplicate your own; a falling-off of active participation by long-time trustees who appear to be 'burned out'; a lack of clear evaluation mechanisms to assess the effectiveness of your services; or a growing body of active volunteers who have language skills relevant to the needs of your clients. Each of these external and internal factors suggests challenges and opportunities that will shape your future. Describe those challenges and opportunities as precisely as you can.

Finally, identify your strengths. What accounts for your most important achievements and successes? Perhaps one factor is an actively involved board of trustees or management committee. Perhaps it is your ability to create wide community networks that allow you to forge alliances and collaborations with other community organisations. Perhaps it is a very high level of skill and expertise in a technically difficult field, such as environmental or employment law. Perhaps it is a level of trust you have built within a 'difficult-to-reach' community, such as asylum-seekers or victims of sexual abuse. Perhaps it is your success in building a broad membership base that gives you loyal financial support year after year. To build on your strengths, you need to define them. Be careful: defining your strengths is not wishful thinking or self-deception, but a matter of isolating tangible factors that have demonstrably contributed to your success.

This segment of your strategic plan analysis might be organised to look something like the outline shown on page 12. Note that 'challenges' and 'opportunities' are not designated separately. People often regard 'challenges' as threats, or weaknesses, and become worried and defensive. Challenges and opportunities are often the same thing: indeed, a challenge can become an opportunity. What you are identifying here are the factors that will shape your future, call for a response, or force you to adapt.

Your responses to the query 'where' should give you an accurate snapshot of your organisation at this moment, a good understanding of the most important issues you face going forward, and a sense of your strengths and needs as you prepare to look ahead.

Whither?

Where are you going? In other words, what will be your response to the challenges and opportunities you have identified?

This portion of the strategic plan helps you articulate a vision for the future. What impact do you think you could have on the lives of your clients or audiences, the quality of life in your community, or the state of the world, in the next few years and beyond? And to achieve that impact, what are your strategic organisational goals for the next three to five years? What are your strategic goals for the more distant future?

11

Remember that each step of the strategic plan builds on what has gone before, so before you look ahead, look back once again at your mission statement. Everything you project for the future must advance your core mission. Occasionally, at this point, an organisation will recognise the need to reconsider its mission statement, in light of the emerging challenges and

---

Strategic Planning Worksheet 3: challenges, opportunities, and strengths

CHALLENGES AND OPPORTUNITIES

1._____

_____

_____

_____

2._____

_____

_____

_____

3._____

_____

_____

_____

etc.

STRENGTHS

1._____

_____

_____

_____

2._____

_____

_____

_____

etc.

---

opportunities it has identified. The classic example is the organisation that has devoted its efforts to the search for a cure for a specific disease; when that cure is achieved, or clearly within reach, the organisation needs to re-examine the rationale for its existence.

Begin with a vision statement. This is a combination of idealistic and practical thinking: your aspirations for a future in which you can fully realise your mission and your aspirations to effect change in the world. For example, an organisation in Cardiff that offers counselling services and referrals to victims of domestic abuse might state as its vision.

> We seek to create a safe, nurturing environment for women who are victims of domestic abuse, in order to assist them to lead secure, healthy, and productive lives. To achieve this vision we aspire to provide a network of refuges throughout South Wales offering temporary protected housing for women and their children and a full range of crisis and long-range support services.

Like your mission statement, this is intended (for the moment) only for internal planning purposes, so keep it simple, direct, and free of rhetoric. And be careful not to overstate your vision: 'a world without AIDS' is of course a world we all long to achieve, but your organisational vision must be framed within the boundaries of your mission (perhaps, 'the ability to reach all youth in Southeast London with a full array of easily accessible, age-appropriate, and culturally tailored information and counselling services designed to prevent the transmission of AIDS').

Now turn more specifically to organisational goals: first short-term goals that could be completed within the next three to five years, then goals for the more distant future. These goals represent concrete, measurable steps toward the achievement of your vision. In the example mentioned above, two short-term goals might be.

> 1. To build a shelter [in a specific town or city] to provide temporary protected housing and around-the-clock crisis services for [X number of] women and children.
> 2. To develop new strategies and programmes of community outreach.

Other goals might address issues of organisational capacity or management: for example, instituting a formal programme of staff training, stabilising operating revenue, expanding the board of trustees, or creating a new administrative structure.

Each short-term goal should be framed as a direct response to challenges and opportunities described in the preceding segment, so that you could put the two worksheets side by side and justify every goal by its 'cause', or origin, in one or more specific challenges or opportunities. And in designating your goals, remember that you have also identified your unique organisational strengths. Goals that build on these strengths are the most likely to be attainable.

Your five-to-ten-year goals will of necessity be less precise, and some of them may seem unlikely or impracticable from where you stand now, but you should nonetheless attempt to describe long-term goals as a way of keeping your feet firmly on the path to becoming 'the best you can be'. For a few organisations, those with a narrowly defined mission, the long-term goal might be simply a restatement of the organisational vision; for most, there may be intermediate steps toward a vision whose achievement is more remote. Eventually, as you approach the point where the attainment of your short-term goals is in sight, you will begin strategic planning all over again, so the horizon is always moving, bringing you closer and closer to your vision of the ideal future.

When you have defined your goals, arrange them in priority order of importance, again reflecting the relative urgency of the challenges and opportunities you have previously identified. Your analysis might look something like the worksheet shown on page 15.

A common question is how many goals should be contained in a strategic plan? For a large, structurally complex organisation like a university, there could be 10 or even 20 or more just for the immediate short-term period, and as long as they all reflect the core mission and are directly responsive to your analysis of challenges and opportunities, there is no inherent problem. However, for a small charity or a young organisation, it is probably best to focus on just a few immediate goals, perhaps three or four, so that your limited resources can be targeted to your most urgent needs.

How?

Now that you have identified goals, you need to decide how you will achieve them. The quick answer is usually 'by raising money', but this is not always, or even most often, the right answer.

Perhaps you have designated as your highest-priority goal the reorientation of your family service programmes to an ageing client population, based on the prediction that within the next three years more than half your clients will be over the age of 40. There are a number of strategies you might consider, alone and in combination. You might decide to reduce some current programmes specifically targeted to children, especially as several other charities that provide youth-oriented services have established themselves in the community over the past few years, and reallocate those resources to services for older people. You might focus on retraining staff and changing your staff and volunteer recruitment policies to acquire more

Strategic Planning Worksheet 4: vision and goals

VISION for your future capacity and achievements as an organisation and your impact on the community (or the world):

_____

_____

_____

_____

_____

SHORT-TERM ORGANISATIONAL GOALS (3–5 YEARS)

Priority 1_____

_____

_____

_____

Priority 2_____

_____

_____

_____

Priority 3_____

_____

_____

_____

etc.

LONG-TERM ORGANISATIONAL GOALS (5–10 YEARS)

Priority 1_____

_____

_____

_____

Priority 2_____

_____

_____

_____

etc.

people with relevant skills. You might set up a formal collaboration with another organisation so that resources targeted to older clients can be shared. Yes, some fundraising might be required, but it would not be your primary strategy.

Even if one of your priority goals addresses financial issues, fundraising might not be the most relevant answer. For example, if a high priority is to wipe out persistent deficits in operating revenue, you might look first at other strategies: more rigorous budgeting and accounting practices, reallocation of resources from under-utilised activities, achievement of efficiencies (thereby savings) in staffing and management, or more emphasis on the development of opportunities for earned revenue (perhaps through increased sales of publications or rentals of space). More aggressive fundraising might be a part of this mix, but not the most important part.

Your analysis of 'how' in the strategic plan might look something like the worksheet shown on page 17.

After you have designated your short-term organisational goals in priority order and analysed the best strategies for achieving them, you will want to assign a timetable and costs to each goal. But we will leave these steps aside for consideration in a later chapter.

With the completion of these analytical exercises and five worksheets, you now have all the basic elements of a strategic plan. Later in this chapter we will consider the relevance of the strategic plan to planning for a capital campaign. But first, let's look briefly at the process for making a strategic plan.

How do you organise the process for strategic planning?

The description of strategic planning on the preceding pages is the bare outline of what can become a fairly complicated and lengthy process, particularly in a large, complex organisation where dozens if not hundreds of people are involved in institutional decision-making. But the process can work well even when it is streamlined and relatively quick, so long as you approach it thoughtfully and with honesty and intellectual rigour.

There is no single correct way to produce a strategic plan, but the process should adhere to some important basic principles.

The planning process should always begin with the authorisation of the board of trustees or management committee, and end with the board's formal endorsement of the strategic plan. This procedure assures that those responsible for the governance of the organisation recognise the authority both of the process and of the plan as the framework for future decisions. You will also note, in the paragraphs below, that the board retains its involvement in the process through the participation of its members in the various stages of analysis and debate.

Strategic Planning Worksheet 5: strategies for short-term organisational goals

Priority	Strategy
Priority 1	1.
	2.
	3.
Priority 2	1.
	2.
	3.
etc.	

You will need a small strategic planning steering committee (sometimes called a long-range planning committee) to shepherd the process, including the collection and preliminary analysis of information and the formulation of draft recommendations. These are the 'worker bees', and the members should be people who will commit time and serious attention to the process as an organisational priority. The committee should have at least one and preferably more representatives from the board or management committee; key members of staff who bring critical expertise on organisational policy, programmes and services, and management; and in appropriate cases, perhaps a volunteer who is involved with the organisation on an ongoing basis.

Strategic planning derives much of its power from the fact that it is a consultative process. Since its purpose is to achieve organisational commitment to a course of action that will affect everyone, an attempt should be made to embrace the entire organisation in the process. In smaller organisations literally everyone can play a role; in larger organisations this would be unwieldy, but there may be ways to reach a broadly representative sample. Meetings at which you consider mission, values, and vision are often appropriate occasions for this wider participation.

At certain points it may be helpful to reach beyond the ranks of the organisation to seek additional expertise and viewpoints, for example, during the assessment of the external environment, where a small committee of outside experts, programme staff, and client representatives might have valuable insight into the needs and expectations of the community. Another often-helpful mechanism is to designate one or two 'task forces' with a brief to focus on principal aspects of the organisation's work, for example, the future of education programmes in a science museum. These ancillary committee structures have the additional benefit of broadening organisational participation in the strategic planning process, particularly by staff and volunteers working on the front lines of your services to clients and the community – often your most trustworthy eyes and ears to the outside world.

As noted earlier, the strategic planning worksheets are sufficient as the foundation for further organisational planning, including the planning of a capital campaign. However, it is customary to turn your worksheets into a more formal presentation for submission to the board of trustees and distribution throughout the organisation. This should not be elaborate – merely a brief prose version of the worksheet outlines – but you may find it useful to append additional documentation, such as a summary of the information you collected for your external and internal assessments, a timeline of meetings and a list of participants, and possibly the worksheets themselves.

Finally, strategic planning is not over when the board adopts the plan. The plan must be evaluated periodically – ideally at least every 18 months – for three inter-related purposes: (1) to measure progress toward each priority goal; (2) to assure that the organisation is not losing focus on its most important priorities and strategies and veering off course; and (3) to take account of unforeseen and unavoidable developments – whether external or internal – that might render some aspects of the plan unworkable or unsuited to a changed set of circumstances. The review should be conducted with the same rigour that governed the original planning process; do not be tempted to deviate from a well-constructed strategic plan without a solid rationale. Your strategic planning steering committee would be the logical body to take on this task, again reaching out to staff, volunteers, and other stakeholders for relevant information on which to base a fair evaluation. The results of the review, and any recommendations for alterations to the strategic plan, should be submitted to the board for analysis and approval.

(For further reading on strategic planning, see the *Further Reading* section at the end of this book.)

Do you need a capital campaign?

Yes, possibly, if your strategic plan tells you that the acquisition of permanent new assets (a building, a major new programme initiative, endowment, or any combination of these) may be the correct strategy to address your organisation's most compelling challenges and opportunities in accordance with its mission and values. No, if your strategic plan tells you that other needs have higher priority, or that other strategies would be more effective in meeting your needs.

Let's go back to that organisation at the beginning of this chapter that wants to build a theatre. How could a strategic planning process inform its decision? Perhaps the process would have revealed that this theatre company was competing for audiences with several recently established university avant-garde theatres; that its potential audience base was becoming more ethnically diverse; that it was running small but persistent operating deficits; but also that its productions were drawing increasing favourable attention in the national arts media. These might have been identified as the company's most compelling challenges and opportunities, giving precedence to audience-building as a more effective and immediately relevant strategy rather than a capital campaign to construct a theatre. Or, the process might have revealed a different set of challenges and opportunities indicating that building its own theatre, and possibly raising endowment to help support it, was this company's most strategically logical next step. Either way, the decision would be based on demonstrated fact and analysis.

Your strategic plan should guide the decision whether to launch a capital campaign and what to include in the campaign. And strategic planning can help support your campaign in other ways.

● The process helps you develop a persuasive message for the public and for your potential donors. It forces you to define your mission and your values succinctly, establishing your unique characteristics and qualities in a competitive fundraising marketplace. It helps you to articulate an inspiring vision for the future, both for the community you serve and for the role your own organisation will play. It provides factual, objective confirmation of the needs you will be asking donors to support.

• Of equal importance, the process of strategic planning helps your organisation muster the will for a campaign. It involves your trustees in making the decision and fosters their commitment to its success. It involves your staff and volunteers and helps convince them of the need to devote some of their energies and attention to high-level fundraising – an activity that can sometimes place great stress on the day-to-day business of the organisation.

If your strategic plan tells you that a capital campaign may be right for you, you still have other hurdles to jump. The next chapters will discuss what you need to do to get ready for a capital campaign, and how to submit the decision to a final test before you move forward.

CHAPTER THREE

Getting ready: defining goals

The first step in planning a capital campaign is to make a rough sketch of what the campaign might look like: what are you raising money for? how much do you need to raise? and how long will the campaign last? None of these decisions can be made with precision at this early stage, but you have to begin somewhere, so educated guesses will have to suffice. Later, you will subject these educated guesses to more rigorous tests before you construct a real campaign plan.

This chapter will take you through the process of defining preliminary campaign goals. Give each topic your best judgement based on the information you have to hand now, but remember, this is a work in progress and you will have ample time to revisit your decisions.

Finally, don't forget the strategic plan! Consult your strategic planning worksheets as you design your campaign. The plan is not a dead document to be relegated to a dusty shelf: it is the guide to your organisation's future. The design of your capital campaign should evolve directly from the content of your strategic plan.

To organise the planning exercises described in this chapter and those that follow, you will need a small campaign planning committee. Often this is a slightly altered version of the strategic planning steering committee (see Chapter 2). You will want to include at least one trustee or member of your management committee so that the link between planning and governance is maintained; you will also want to include key senior staff who bring expertise in programme, finance, fundraising, and administration. As with the strategic planning process itself, campaign planning should reach out to involve as many people within the organisation as possible – especially those responsible for the day-to-day operation of your programmes and services, but you will need a small group of leaders to keep the process moving forward.

Defining goals: what are you raising money for?

Even though the distinguishing feature of a capital campaign is its focus on creating permanent new assets, your capital campaign will become the umbrella for all your fundraising efforts – the context in which you present all your needs as an integrated package.

It is true that some capital campaigns are run as self-contained appeals, separate from and parallel to the organisation's 'normal' fundraising for operations. This carries some risks, for example, that some of your current donors may 'jump ship' to support an exciting new capital project and leave a hole in your operating budget. It also can result in a wasteful duplication and poor coordination of effort; and most important, it prevents you from taking advantage of the power of an integrated presentation, in which all of your fundraising needs are mutually reinforced within the larger picture of your mission, vision, and organisational priorities. In this book we will follow the model of the all-encompassing capital campaign, incorporating your capital, programme, and other operating needs within a single structure.

Your first task, therefore, is to define the substance (the subject matter) of your campaign goals. Over what period? For purposes of this initial planning exercise let's say about two to three years for a small organisation with just a few campaign goals, and about five to six years for a large organisation with a longer list of goals. (Intensive fundraising, of the kind you will undertake in a capital campaign, is often more productive when compressed into a relatively short period than when it is stretched out over a longer period.) Here are some examples of the kinds of goals, derived from the strategic plan, that might be incorporated into a capital campaign at a small university:

- a major programme initiative, for example, the creation of an entirely new university department devoted to Asian studies;
- endowment to support the new department, including several endowed faculty chairs;
- a new student residential building;
- several new projects and the expansion of some existing projects (not involving the creation of new capital assets) that address the priority needs of other university departments: for example, a programme to encourage more women to study science, or additional staff and equipment for the university library;
- operating support for all the ongoing scholarly, educational, and community activities the university provides, including both existing activities and the additional operating costs of new assets as they are created.

The goals for a smaller organisation would be more modest. A community youth services charity that has been operating out of 'borrowed' church basements might specify, for example:

- acquisition and refurbishment of a building to create a community youth services centre;
- operating support for all of its youth services programmes, which will be consolidated into the new centre;
- a pilot project to establish new services for children with disabilities.

Whether the list is long or short, it will achieve thematic coherence as the 'story' of your capital campaign because it is derived from the mission, vision, priorities, and strategies defined in your strategic plan.

Estimating costs

Now you need to begin working with numbers. Each campaign goal has a cost, so first you must determine the total cost, and then you must analyse how much of the cost will be supported by fundraising. At this early stage, it will be difficult to define costs accurately. Your initial estimates may be rough, but what you want to achieve now is a sense of scale. Will your campaign have a target of £1,000,000, £5,000,000, £50,000,000, or £100,000,000?

As you make your first effort to estimate total costs, without determining what portion of the total will come from fundraising, let's look at some important issues you need to consider.

New capital assets: buildings

The costs of construction and renovation projects are very difficult to fix in advance, and are famous, or perhaps infamous, for exceeding original estimates. Have you identified a site, and do you know how much it will cost to acquire it? Do you have a design for the new facility, and was it prepared and priced by reputable professional architects, designers, and construction managers? Have you worked with these professionals before, or do you know other organisations that have? How detailed is your initial design? Does it account for all the elements, including internal finishes and equipment, that could drive your costs up substantially? Have you built a line into your construction budget for contingencies such as unanticipated overruns on budgets and schedules?

Do you know how long planning, design, and construction will take? Even based on preliminary, incomplete information, you should try to project when you will need money, and how much, for different phases of the project: planning and design, various stages of construction, final furnishing and equipment. Do you have a realistic target date for opening the facility? This is the date from which you will need to support the operating expenses of the new building (programme costs, as well as heat, light, telecommunications, etc.). Have you analysed and estimated these costs? Often, but not always, the opening of a new building coincides with the end of the campaign; what you are trying to assess now is how much of these new operating expenses will need to be raised during the period of the campaign.

Preparing the budget for a construction or renovation project is a technically demanding exercise, and not for amateurs. The consequences of underestimating the costs of a building can be disastrous for your organisation, depleting resources that should be supporting your programmes and services, straining your fundraising capacity, and burdening you with deficits for years to come. This is an area in which you need to make an up-front investment to assure that you have expert professional guidance.

New capital assets: programme initiatives

Let's go back to the example of the new university department, or the example mentioned in an earlier chapter, the replication of an existing programme in another city. The process of estimating these costs should feel more familiar, since you will employ the same analysis you normally use for budgeting your current programmes. You will have to calculate both the initial and the ongoing costs of space, staff, administration and overhead, and materials and equipment during the period of the campaign, so you need to set a target start-up date. Also be alert to other possible costs: for instance, will your new initiative require a financial investment in advance planning and preparation, or do you plan to test your new initiative on a pilot basis before launching it at full scale?

New capital assets: endowment

It is hard to establish a goal for endowment because there is no obvious price tag. There are really two questions to consider: what percentage of your ongoing operating expenses should you strive to support by endowment, and how much endowment can you 'afford' to raise in light of other needs?

There are two types of endowment. An unrestricted endowment fund can be used to support any and all aspects of your activities, including general administration. A restricted endowment fund is targeted at a stated purpose. Sometimes this is defined narrowly, such as an endowed faculty chair in English literature or a fund solely for the acquisition of rare books for a library. Or it can be defined more broadly, perhaps as a general fund for educational programmes in a museum or scholarship support for needy students at a private school. Many campaigns that include endowment incorporate a mix of unrestricted and restricted endowment funds into their goals.

In Chapter 1 we noted that most endowments draw revenue for operating expenses at a rate of 4–6%. At 5%, this means that an endowment fund of £1,000,000 will produce £50,000 annually for operating expenses; £2,000,000 will produce £100,000; and the yields will increase in proportion as the capital fund increases. It is difficult to say how much endowment is 'enough', but you might posit a given percentage of your total operating expenses as the endowment goal. An organisation that starts its campaign with no endowment might set a goal of supporting just 5–10% of its operating costs; an organisation that already has some endowment might try to increase that percentage by an additional 10–15%.

Having said that endowment has no price tag in the way that construction projects and new programmes have tangible costs, there is in fact an 'opportunity cost'. As noted earlier, £500,000 raised for operating needs is £500,000 of operating revenue in the till; £500,000 raised for endowment will place only about £25,000 in the till per year. Thus, you may have to assess the opportunity to raise a given amount of money for immediate expenditure against the opportunity to secure a reliable stream of revenue to support a portion of your expenses in the future. Can you afford the trade-off? You probably cannot answer this question until you have appraised all your revenue sources (including fundraising capacity – a topic we will address in the next chapter).

Meanwhile, here are some important issues to keep in mind as you consider whether to raise endowment and, if so, how much.

Should you try to raise endowment?

• Endowment is the most permanent of all capital assets. An endowment is a fund 'in perpetuity' – and perpetuity is a very long time! Therefore, a young organisation, one with little history and an uncertain future, or one whose mission might alter radically with changing circumstances, will not have the credibility or indeed any reason to raise endowment. As you approach the point where you and your funders can envision a long, reasonably stable, future, it may be time to consider building an endowment to help support and secure that future.

• Raising funds for endowment may displace your current operating support. That is, you may be unable to bear the cost of raising endowment unless you are absolutely sure that you can meet your immediate needs for current operating revenue.

• Endowments are typically received as large gifts paid out regularly over a period of many years. The capital must usually be invested for at least one full financial year before its yield can be retrieved and budgeted for operating support. Therefore, unless you can expect substantial endowment funds to be pledged and fully paid early in your campaign, it is a prudent strategy to assume that endowment gifts will not be producing substantial operating revenue until the campaign is very near its close or has actually ended.

• Restricted endowment is likely to be tricky. If the restriction is too narrowly focussed, the life of the endowment may outlast its purpose, and you may find yourself renegotiating with a donor years into the future. Therefore, you should be certain that restricted endowments are sufficiently flexible to take into account reasonably predictable changes in the organisation's structure, stated goals or scope of activities.

• Campaigns frequently designate a goal for restricted endowment to help support a new building or new programme initiative. This is an effective way to provide for some of the increased operating costs that your organisation will have to support as it expands its permanent assets.

• Occasionally, an organisation will run a campaign in which endowment is the only capital goal. This makes sense for an organisation – usually a large organisation – that has recently experienced a rapid, substantial expansion, creating major capital assets and programme enhancements that will need to be supported into the indefinite future. While raising endowment may not be as 'sexy' as constructing a theatre, building a museum, or launching a new university department, an endowment campaign can be very appealing because it can offer imaginative naming opportunities that will perpetuate donors' names 'in perpetuity'. (Just think of all those museums, colleges, professorships, hospitals, and libraries endowed by benefactors, sometimes centuries ago, whose names are still familiar to us today.)

• Taking into account all these factors, including opportunity costs and your ability to cover current operating needs, your endowment goals, if any, should be guided by the strategic plan. If the plan has designated the achievement of financial stability and security as one of your highest priorities, endowment should be considered as a component of your campaign if at all feasible.

Operating costs

Recall that your capital campaign will encompass fundraising for all your needs, not just new capital assets. A large portion of your campaign, possibly the largest, will be for operating costs, known in fundraising terminology as the 'operating base'.

For purposes of this analysis we will consider your operating base as the total costs of running your day-to-day activities during the entire course of the campaign. To quantify your operating base, you need to make a preliminary estimate of the probable duration of your campaign and then do the following.

• On a year-by-year basis, project the annual operating costs of your continuing 'core activities', on the assumption that these will continue for the period of the campaign. If, in accordance with your strategic plan, you expect to reduce or eliminate some of these core activities, this should be reflected in your projections.

• Look at any time-limited projects that you are supporting now, and determine whether you plan to renew these through the period of the campaign. If so, add these costs to your year-by-year analysis.

• Go back to the sections above on the costs of buildings and new programme initiatives, and slot in the operating costs of these new capital assets at the appropriate points in your year-by-year analysis.

• Add in the costs of incremental (non-capital) programme enhancements and new time-limited projects you plan to launch during the period of the campaign in furtherance of your strategic plan; designate target starting dates, and add these new operating costs into your year-by-year analysis.

• Don't forget 'hidden' costs, especially those for general administration and overhead. These should be included in all core and project operating budgets.

• Finally, do not forget that if you plan to finance any portion of your capital projects through a loan, you need to add annual costs for repayment into your operating base.

Note that at this stage you are not distinguishing between operating costs that you support through unrestricted operating revenue (such as your annual fund) and costs that you support through restricted contracts or grants, nor are you deciding how much of these costs will be supported by fundraising as opposed to other sources of income – that will come next. What you should have at the end of this exercise is a table that looks roughly like the sample shown on page 28, using a five-year campaign as an example.

Sample analysis of operating base						
	Year 1	Year 2	Year 3	Year 4	Year 5	Total
Core/continuing activities	£100,000	£105,000	£110,000	£115,000	£120,000	£550,000
Time-limited projects	£ 75,000	£ 80,000	£ 50,000	£ 50,000	£ 50,000	£305,000
Operation of new assets	–	–	£ 25,000	£ 30,000	£ 80,000	£135,000
Total	£175,000	£185,000	£185,000	£195,000	£250,000	£990,000

This analysis tells a story. This organisation will need nearly one million pounds to support its operating base over the period of a five-year campaign, but the components of that base will change. It looks as if core activities will continue on an even course, the costs rising gradually in line with inflation. However, some time-limited special projects will be reduced in the third year, perhaps to be replaced, in part, by a new capital programme initiative that will start up that year, and the operations of a refurbished building show up in the fifth year. When the campaign is over, this organisation will have increased its annual operating base from £175,000 to £250,000. Your analysis must similarly reflect the evolution of your operating base over the duration of your campaign. And you need to be aware that this higher operating base must be sustained in the years after your campaign ends.

Campaign costs

The final segment of your preliminary cost analysis focuses on the campaign itself. There are costs associated with planning and running a capital campaign: expenses incurred before the campaign starts (for example, for a feasibility study – a subject addressed in Chapter 5); expansion of fundraising, marketing, and communications staff; publications and presentation materials; plaques to acknowledge campaign donors; events and activities related to the cultivation and stewardship of donors; and possibly even the acquisition of new donor record or accounting systems that will allow you to manage your campaign efficiently.

In a sense, introducing this topic now puts the cart before the horse, since until you have read through this entire book you cannot accurately anticipate all the types of costs that might be involved. At this point you may want to look quickly through the section entitled *Building organisa-*

tional capacity in Chapter 4 and make a tentative list of campaign planning and management needs that have costs attached. It can also be helpful to consult friends and colleagues in other organisations that have run capital campaigns. People are always happy to share their 'war stories,' and you might get at least a rough idea of the campaign-related costs that you need to estimate.

Fundraising goals

You are now at a point where you can make an inventory of capital, operating, and campaign costs and a preliminary, rough estimate of the total costs for each year of your campaign. Put all the information into a simple table, similar to the one you developed for the operating base. Here is how such a table might be organised for a five-year campaign.

Preliminary cost analysis						
	Year 1	Year 2	Year 3	Year 4	Year 5	Total
Buildings (capital)						
Programme initiatives (capital)						
Endowment (capital)						
Total operating base						
Campaign costs						
Total						

Now you need to determine what portion of these costs will be met by fundraising, and what portion can be supported from other sources. How much of your revenue is currently derived from sources other than fundraising? With additional effort, how much more revenue could you derive from sources other than fundraising?

Here are some of the alternative revenue sources you should examine:

- Earned income, including the sale of publications, fees for services provided, ticket sales for performances or public programmes, sales in museum or charity shops and cafés, rental of space to individuals or businesses for private events, admission fees, and tuition.

- Revenue from existing endowment.

- Other steady income streams, such as rental of office space on your premises to another organisation, interest from bank accounts, or revenue from other investments.

- Ongoing statutory funding and renewable contracts for services provided for a public purpose.

- Reallocation of resources from activities that will be reduced or eliminated.

- Memberships. (Note that many membership programmes are simply a vehicle for charitable donations, for example, a child poverty charity whose members give annual contributions, receiving perhaps an occasional newsletter. However, some membership schemes are structured and marketed to allow members to 'buy' certain privileges and services, for example, the Friends programme in a museum that may provide free admission and exhibition previews to members, a Friends Room where members can purchase a light lunch, and substantial discounts in the museum shop. This is usually considered a form of earned income.)

Determine all the sources of non-fundraising revenue you currently receive. If it is feasible to project an increase in these non-fundraising sources over the course of your campaign, increase the numbers. Allocate this revenue to appropriate costs in your preliminary cost analysis table, but wherever possible, apply non-fundraising revenue to the operating base, which is the most critical and often the most difficult to sustain during a capital campaign.

Recalculate the numbers in your table by subtracting revenues derived from non-fundraising sources from your costs. Now incorporate these numbers into a new table entitled *Preliminary fundraising goals* (see the table at the beginning of Chapter 4). In the following two chapters we will examine how to decide whether these numbers represent feasible fundraising goals for a capital campaign, and at a later stage you will adjust your year-by-year fundraising goals to match your fundraising strategies (see Chapter 9). As you proceed to the next steps in planning, continue to study and refine your estimates of costs and non-fundraising revenues, so that by the time you make a final decision to launch a campaign you will have an accurate picture of your projected costs and a reliable assessment of your fundraising goals.

Developing the case

But first, you have one more task to complete in establishing your goals. You need to articulate the case for your campaign.

Eventually, you will publish a formal case statement that presents the justification for your campaign to the public. Now you only need a rough draft of a case statement, first as the basis for discussions within the organisation that will build commitment to a campaign, and later as the basis for 'testing the waters' with key stakeholders and potential supporters in the community.

Return to your strategic plan. Start with a succinct restatement of your mission, values, strengths, and vision to express clearly who you are, why you do what you do, and what you envision as the future for your organisation and for the community it serves. Then describe the purposes of your campaign, justified as responses to the challenges and opportunities identified in the strategic plan. Don't couch your goals as a description of your own needs but rather as the means of addressing a societal problem or community need. ('We need a new building because our rented space is too small and is falling about our ears' is not as compelling as 'We will build an attractive arts and cultural centre capable of serving the city's growing community of recent immigrants from Africa'.) Show how your organisational goals fit together to achieve, or move closer to, the vision you have portrayed. End with a brief outline of the campaign's preliminary fundraising goals.

Like everything else at this early stage of planning, this draft case statement is a work in progress. You will re-examine and refine it as the campaign plan itself is examined and refined. Try to limit this first draft to two to three pages, so that you don't get bogged down in rhetoric and slogans. Discipline yourself by keeping a clear link to your strategic plan, as a reminder that your campaign is a necessary response to issues, challenges, and opportunities that have been defined in a rigorous process of analysis and planning.

Now, with preliminary costs and fundraising goals and a draft case statement in hand, it is time to move to the other side of the equation: your ability to find the necessary resources to achieve your campaign goals.

CHAPTER FOUR

Getting ready: identifying resources

The last chapter took you through the process of defining campaign goals, ending with a chart of estimated fundraising goals that should look something like this:

Preliminary fundraising goals						
	Year 1	Year 2	Year 3	Year 4	Year 5	Total
Buildings (capital)						
Programme initiatives (capital)						
Endowment (capital)						
Total operating base						
Campaign costs						
Total						

This chapter will help you determine whether you have sufficient resources to meet these goals. The exercise is useful because it will demonstrate clearly the work you need to do to acquire the resources necessary for a successful capital campaign.

Leadership

Organisational leadership is your most precious asset. Without it, the odds of meeting your campaign goals are against you. With it, you may be able to achieve all the other resources you need.

You can look for leadership in a variety of places. Certainly a knowledgeable, charismatic, energetic chief executive is a natural leader. A core group of staff members, each expert in their own field and able to work together as a team, is an invaluable source of leadership. Volunteer workers and clients, because of their life experiences and personal talents and skills, can emerge as organisational leaders. But the leadership we will examine here, the one most crucial to your campaign, is your governing body: the board of trustees or management committee.

Board responsibilities

The responsibilities of governance, embodied in your board or management committee, can be summarised most simply as follows:

- to establish overall organisational policy;
- to preserve organisational integrity and well-being;
- to ensure adequate organisational resources.

This last point, ensuring adequate resources, creates the link to board involvement in fundraising. If fundraising is a significant source of financial support, then the board bears ultimate responsibility for its success.

Trustees as fundraising leaders

Here are some of the ways in which board members advance an organisation's fundraising activities:

- by establishing the purposes and goals for fundraising

- by making a financial contribution commensurate with ability

- by identifying, and opening doors to, potential donors

- by asking for gifts on the organisation's behalf

- by participating in cultivation, fundraising, and donor stewardship events.

Let's look at each of these functions in turn, and consider their relevance to a capital campaign.

Through their participation in strategic planning (see Chapter 2) and campaign planning (see Chapter 3), board members individually and collectively shape the organisation's fundraising priorities. We have noted that the strategic plan is formally adopted by the board. Similarly, at the end of the campaign planning process, the board will authorise the final plan, thereby establishing the organisation's fundraising goals and formally launching the campaign. And with this action, the board implicitly also assumes responsibility for holding the organisation to the agreed priorities and for assuring that adequate resources will be made available to run a successful campaign.

Board members should be expected to support the organisation financially to the best of their ability. This assertion makes some people uncomfortable. 'Our trustees volunteer enormous amounts of time; they don't expect to be asked for money too.' 'Our trustees are as poor as our clients; they don't have any money to give.' 'We would lose trustees if we asked them for money.' These objections are understandable, but the truth is that your attempts to obtain money from outside sources will be far more credible when the people most immediately responsible for the organisation's well-being (the board) have contributed first. The key is proportionality. A gift of £5 from a trustee who is on benefit or £50 from a trustee who is a social worker is commensurate with a gift of £500,000 from a trustee who is an investment banker. You will be asking campaign donors to give generously to meet extraordinary needs, but your case will be less compelling if your board has not done its part first.

Through their work, social life, family, going back even to their childhood and education, board members have networks: circles of friends, associates, and acquaintances that could yield potential donors to your campaign. With encouragement and coaching, your trustees may be able to identify and make introductions to these contacts.

The request for a campaign gift is particularly powerful when it comes from a trustee. This is another scary thought for many people: 'I'll do anything to help except ask for money'. But there are ways in which trustees can be supported so that asking does not have to be an ordeal. (See section entitled *Support: the key to volunteer success* in Chapter 6.) It is an axiom of fundraising that people give to people, not to institutions. Requests from trustees have unique credibility in the eyes of potential donors (another reason that trustees need to contribute first, to validate that credibility), and gifts obtained with the active participation of trustees also help to strengthen the board's pride and commitment to the success of the campaign.

Throughout your campaign you will be hosting events to cultivate, solicit, and thank donors. The participation of board members, once again, gives these occasions special authority through the visible presence of the people who bear primary responsibility for the organisation's future. Here they can act as advocates for and representatives of the organisation's mission, values, vision, and needs.

If you would like to learn more about the roles of trustees, including their responsibilities for fundraising, see the *Further Reading* section at the end of this book.

Assessing leadership potential

Knowing that the success of your campaign may rely heavily upon the commitment and participation of your board, you need to examine, at an early stage, its leadership potential. Setting aside sentiments of gratitude and loyalty, make a dispassionate inventory of the talents, skills, networks, and enthusiasm of your board of trustees or management committee, and assess the likelihood that they can be persuaded to put those assets to use in a vigorous fundraising effort.

Make a list of your board members and start jotting down relevant qualities and facts. Here is a sampling of the attributes you might be looking for.

• A gift for public speaking. These trustees can be charismatic advocates for your organisation at campaign events and in public forums.

• A successful business or professional career. Such people usually have wide networks that can be plumbed as sources of substantial gifts, and their effectiveness in business or a profession usually means that they know how to approach peers and colleagues with confidence.

• A reputation for gracious entertaining. Such trustees can host cultivation, fundraising, and stewardship events, and they probably also have extensive social contacts.

• Experience in running another voluntary organisation or a business. This might contribute valuable expertise to your strategic planning and campaign planning.

• Money. The relevance is obvious. Many organisations do not have wealthy boards, but it is important to have some idea of the net worth of your board and its overall giving potential.

• Above all, passion for the cause and the motivation to do what needs to be done. Energy and an open mind can translate into a willingness to learn new skills and put them to use for the organisation's benefit.

What other attributes, and their applications to campaign fundraising, can you add to this list? What are your board's greatest strengths?

Now take a look at one trustee in particular: the board chair. The chair is the leader of leaders. That person will galvanise the motivation, zeal, and commitment of the other trustees, set the pace and the example, and probably be the most publicly visible member of the board. What qualities and potential does your chair bring to this assignment?

Finally, a key consideration is the relationship of your chief executive to the board and to the chair in particular. A chief executive and a board chair who can work constructively together and complement each other's strong points make an unbeatable team.

Developing board leadership

Having catalogued your board's skills, strengths, and potential, you need to look for what is missing. An honest assessment of your board's weaknesses is the necessary prelude to board development in anticipation of a capital campaign.

It is futile to expect 100% board involvement. There will always be some trustees whose value and contributions to the organisation's welfare lie outside the realm of a fundraising campaign. There may be some trustees who are virtually inert for any purpose, but who cannot be retired and replaced at the moment. You should not focus on 'hopeless cases', but rather try to define the skills and strengths you need on your board to run a successful campaign.

Sometimes these missing strengths can be developed within the existing board. More often, the period before a campaign is an opportunity to recruit new trustees with the strengths you need. It is common for an organisation to increase the size of its board or management committee in preparation for a campaign, with the specific intent of filling in the leadership gaps. Just a few new members, chosen deliberately for the skills they will bring to the campaign, can re-invigorate a tired or timid board and substantially increase your leadership capacity.

The question sometimes arises whether major donors and 'hot prospects' should be invited to join the board. There are pros and cons. Your biggest donors, those who have made substantial investments in the past and on whom you will rely to give generously to the campaign, can infuse new zest and motivate other board members and donors who are pondering the level of their own contributions. On the other hand, a major donor who has little interest in the broader responsibilities of governance, who brings no special skills, or who might even be obstructive is a poor candidate for board membership. Certainly you want to be wary of recruiting wealthy people to your board as 'window dressing', without knowing whether they are ready to make a substantial commitment to the work of the organisation.

You also need to be aware that the prospect of a campaign may scare away a few of your current trustees. This can feel like a defeat, but it is simply a by-product of organisational change. If the decision to undertake a campaign arises out of a thoughtful strategic planning process, this means that change is inevitable, possibly including change in the composition of your board. Members who resign because they feel unable to participate in a campaign should not be regarded as failures, but should be encouraged to serve the organisation in other roles that may be more comfortable.

It is also possible that preparations for a campaign will lead to the selection of a new chair. This is not uncommon, and again, it should not be interpreted as a rejection of, or by, the current chair. If it is clear what will be required of the chair in a capital campaign, and if it is clear that new leadership is needed, the change must be made in the organisation's best interests.

Board development takes time. That is why it is necessary to assess your leadership potential at the very beginning of the campaign planning process.

Finally, remember the words that introduced this discussion: organisational leadership is your most precious asset. Acknowledge the significance of board leadership by being willing to delay your campaign until you have the leadership you need.

Funding potential: donor base

We noted in Chapter 1 that campaigns risk failure when it is not clear in advance whether the fundraising goals can be met. You really do have to know that you can complete the campaign even before you begin it. Campaign fundraising will challenge your current capacity to support 'business as usual', and therefore you need to see how far you can push your fundraising potential.

You have established preliminary fundraising goals. Where will the money come from?

Begin with the obvious: the individuals, trusts, companies, and government sources most likely to support the campaign are those that already know you, value your work, and have made an investment in your organisation. Many of your largest campaign gifts will probably come from these sources. Therefore, the first place to look is your current donor base. You need to determine how close you can come to your fundraising goals by pushing your current donor base to its outer limits.

This is a painstaking exercise, but worth the trouble. At the end you will have not only an assessment of the potential of your donor base, but the first draft of an actual fundraising plan. Your aim is to match your donor base against your total fundraising goal, and against each campaign component within that goal.

Starting with your largest donors and working down, make a chart that lists all current and recent donors – say, any donors who have made gifts within the last three years. (Don't forget to include government grants, and, of course, those members of your board who are current donors.) Then, keeping in mind each donor's history and what you know about the donor's interests, net worth and current circumstances, what is your best guess about the purpose and amount (lowest/highest) you might anticipate in campaign support? Your chart should have separate columns to record the following information:

- donor name
- amount, date, and purpose of last gift/grant received
- total amount received since the year of the donor's first gift, and purpose/s
- lowest potential support for the campaign: amount and purpose/s
- highest potential support for the campaign: amount and purpose/s.

The table on page 39 shows how this chart might be set up. If you have a large donor base, prepare a separate chart for each type of donor source: charitable trusts, individuals, companies, and government grants.

As you work your way through descending levels of support, you will reach donors of relatively small amounts where it is impracticable to consider them individually. It is fine to assess these donors who share common characteristics as a group: for example, if you have 200 donors who give £100 or less in operating support every year, you can project your ability to maintain or increase the level of support from this group as a whole.

There is nothing mechanistic about this exercise; projections of future giving can be based on differing interpretations of known facts. You might, for instance, be considering a major individual donor:

Example 1:

Lady A, who has substantial inherited wealth, has donated £50,000 each year for the last five years, all targeted to various services for young children, plus £5,000 each year for general operating support, giving a total of £275,000. Your campaign includes a major new children's initiative and an endowment for children's programmes. Can you project a gift from Lady A of £750,000–£1,000,000 or even more for these purposes? On the other hand, you have just learned that Lady A has joined the board of another children's charity in the city, so she may decide to shift the focus of her support to this organisation. In that case, what amount would you project? These queries can suggest your highest and lowest estimated projections for Lady A.

Assessment of donor base

Name	Last gift: date/amount/purpose	Total giving and purposes	Low campaign projection: amount/purpose	High campaign projection: amount/purpose
Donor A				
Donor B				
Donor C				
Donor D				
Donor E				
etc.				

Example 2:

Company ABC sponsored one of your musical performance series two years ago with a gift of £20,000. Since then, ABC has opened two new manufacturing facilities in the region, its profits and the value of its stock have increased significantly, and it has been sponsoring a lot of local arts events. Also, a member of your board knows the chief executive of ABC very well. What could you project as the highest potential support from ABC for the new theatre you are planning to build?

Example 3:

You have been receiving approximately £200,000 in small donations each year for the last five years through your 'save the environment' direct mail appeals. One of your strategies for increasing operating support is to get this loyal base of donors to increase the amounts they give through more frequent direct mail and telephone appeals that highlight new environmental dangers and emerging issues. What are the lowest and highest amounts you can project from this existing donor base for the period of your capital campaign?

At this point in the exercise, you should not worry if your projections are somewhat fuzzy. You will have the opportunity to subject them to closer scrutiny and correction later. Right now you are seeking, once again, a rough sense of scale. Add up the 'low projection' column; and add up the 'high projection' column. Is either of these figures even remotely within sight of your fundraising goals? Look at how the total figures break down by campaign component. Do you seem to have a lot of prospects for your building fundraising goal, but very few for your endowment goal? (A hint: legacies and bequests are often a useful component of an endowment campaign, although these gifts cannot be counted at full face value as a contribution toward your goal since the funds will not be received until some time in the future.)

There is no hard and fast rule to tell you how close these early projections should be to your goals. If the gap is very large, your first question should be, why? Does your current donor base have the capacity to give more? If so, there are many things you can do to get to know these donors better, help them get to know you better, and motivate them to increase their contributions to a much higher level. But it may be that your current donor base is, for the most part, already giving what it can give. For example, the X, Y, and Z Trusts, which have been loyal supporters, do not make any grants much larger than the ones they have made to you. Lady A does not give any other organisation nearly as much as she has given you, and it is public knowledge that the family wealth has been poured into the upkeep of the ancestral estate. If your donor base does not have much additional capacity, then you must count on raising support from an entirely new pool of donors.

Funding potential: new prospects

A capital campaign is a wonderful opportunity to broaden your circle of donors. The publicity that precedes and accompanies the progress of your campaign (see Chapter 7) may attract the attention of a new pool of prospects; your expanded scope of activities and capabilities, supported by the new capital assets you are creating, may match the interests of a new pool of prospects.

Who are these new prospects? Most likely, they are already somewhere within your orbit, even if they have not yet offered financial support. Here are some of the places you might look for new prospects:

Potential prospect pool

- Trusts and government grant programmes that fund the kinds of new needs described in your campaign goals.

- Donors to other organisations with similar or complementary missions.

- Anyone on your mailing lists to receive newsletters and publicity materials.

- Alumni and past recipients of your services.

- Anyone who has purchased tickets to your performances or public lectures.

- Companies and businesses that have a presence in your community, especially those that have arrived or expanded recently and are seeking to create a profile of 'good corporate citizenship'.

- Individuals and companies known to members of your board or volunteers.

- Individuals and companies known to your current donors.

- Volunteers and ex-volunteers.

- Board members and ex-board members who are not current contributors.

What additional categories can you think of?

The most viable new prospects are unlikely to be complete strangers; you probably already have some connection, however tenuous. Nothing is impossible, and yes, the stranger could turn up at your door with bags of money in hand, but it is dangerous to count on such fairy tale endings. Your best new prospects are already in your peripheral vision, and now need to be brought into the inner circle.

Start doing some prospect research. (See the *Further Reading* section at the end of this book for publications on donor and prospect research.) Start making lists. Set up a new chart, this time as an exercise to project gifts from new prospects, with columns to record the following information:

- prospect name;
- known interests, personal connections, and other relevant facts that suggest a potential contribution to your organisation;
- estimate of net worth, size of gifts to other organisations, and other facts that suggest the level of support of which this prospect may be capable;
- highest potential support for the campaign: amount and purpose/s;
- discounted projection for support of the campaign.

The table on page 43 shows what this chart might look like. Again, it may be easier to organise your new prospect analysis by making separate lists for each type of donor source.

A word of explanation about the 'discounted projection' column. It is good to set your sights high and be optimistic in projecting the highest potential support from each prospect, but then you need to inject a dose of realism, recognizing that you will fall short or fail completely with a certain percentage of new prospects no matter how promising they may look initially. Most experienced fundraisers discount their prospect projections substantially, designating only 25–30% of the highest amount unless they can make a convincing case for more. In fact, for many prospects it is wise to put '0' as your discounted projection – an acknowledgement that you simply do not have enough information at this point to project any amount with confidence.

As before, you may treat some new prospects as affiliated groups. To use the earlier example of annual £100 donors: can you project not just an increased level of giving by the current donors in this category, but can you also recruit a significant number of new prospects to this category through intensified direct mail and publicity efforts?

Now add up the figures in the 'discounted projection' column. How much of the gap has been filled between your current donor base

Assessment of donor base

Name	Interests/personal connections	Assets/gifts to other organisations	High campaign projection: amount/purpose	Discounted campaign projection
Prospect A				
Prospect B				
Prospect C				
Prospect D				
Prospect E				
etc.				

projections and your fundraising goals? Does it look as if a reasonable assessment of support from new prospects can move you substantially closer to your goals? Have you made progress not only toward the total, but also toward each component goal of the campaign?

One of the great values of this exercise is that it may justify a major investment in prospect cultivation. If you are convinced that there is indeed a rich source of untapped support, your campaign is the perfect opportunity to mine this source. You should consider delaying your campaign to allow time for the intensive cultivation of new prospects, if it appears that this could result in substantial additional campaign support.

You are now ready to make a preliminary assessment of your funding potential from current donors and new prospects combined. Add these two sets of projections together. Does the total fall so far from your goals that it is doubtful you can mount a successful campaign – or at least, the campaign as it is now envisaged? Do you need to do more new prospect research? What additional cultivation efforts, with your current donor base and with new prospects, might close the gap? Are there areas of the campaign that don't seem to have enough support, and if so, how can you remedy that? Do you need to press your trustees to scrutinise their networks more closely; do you need new trustees with wider networks? What strategies can you adopt to expand your funding potential?

At this stage there is often still a gap between your funding assessment and your goals. How large a gap is acceptable? How much can you leave to chance and good luck? The most prudent advice is, not much. Many of your current donors will rise to the challenge, the campaign will expand your reach into a pool of new prospects, but there will also be disappointments. By the time you make the final decision to move forward, you should have identified reasonably likely sources for at least 90% of your goal; 95% is better; and the best scenario is to project that you can 'over-fund' your campaign by 5–10% as insurance that you will reach your goals and possibly even surpass them. Some campaigns actually do raise more than initially anticipated, and revise their goals upward to take advantage of the funding momentum they have created.

Gift tables

So far you have focused on the effort to match the total of your fundraising goals with the total of potential support from your donor base and new prospects. Now you need an overall picture of the funding mix. Suppose you are planning a campaign with a goal of £10,000,000. You could reach the goal with two gifts of £5,000,000 or 10,000 gifts of £1,000; either way, the arithmetic works, but neither looks like a sensible fundraising plan!

We use tools called gift tables to project the number and size of gifts necessary to meet a stated fundraising goal. There is no single prescribed pattern, but in general we are looking at three categories (the percentages given here are only approximations):

• a few very large gifts and grants at the top, cumulatively comprising as much as 40–45% of the fundraising goal;

• several descending levels of substantial gifts in the middle, cumulatively comprising perhaps another 45–50% of the goal;

• a broad base of smaller gifts at the bottom to reach 100%.

A gift table (sometimes called a gift pyramid when it is drawn in pyramidal rather than tabular form) gives you a different perspective on your campaign plan by suggesting the mix of gifts you will need to reach your goal. The top levels represent a pool of 'lead gifts' – the largest, pace-setting gifts, by which a relatively few donors account for a significant proportion of the total. Lead gifts not only move the counter substantially forward toward the goal; they also create strong momentum, engender confidence that the goal can be achieved, and thereby encourage other donors to make their own investments in a winning cause. (The word 'lead' refers to the size and not to the timing of the gift. It is not necessary for all lead gifts to be received at the beginning of the campaign, but all the reasonably likely prospects for lead gifts should be identified.) You can see on the sample gift tables on page 46 what a struggle it would be to raise £10,000,000 in increments of £100,000 or £200,000, and how unconvincing such a strategy would appear to your donors.

But the middle ground is critical too. There is still a huge space to fill on our sample gift tables with many gifts ranging from £50,000 to £500,000. As any experienced fundraiser will tell you, it can take as much work to bring in a £50,000 gift as a £5,000,000 gift, so this middle ground represents a wide and varied pool of donors who will require a great deal of attention and effort. The lowest levels may encompass hundreds or even thousands of individuals, representing the campaign's broadest reach into your community and constituency.

Here is one way to draw a gift table for a £10,000,000 campaign, working from the organisation's assessment of its donor base and new prospects.

Sample gift table 1	
1 gift @ £2,500,000	total £2,500,000
2 gifts @ £1,000,000	total £2,000,000
3 gifts @ £500,000	total £1,500,000
5 gifts @ £250,000	total £1,250,000
10 gifts @ £100,000	total £1,000,000
20 gifts @ £50,000	total £1,000,000
30 gifts @ £10,000	total £300,000
60 gifts @ £5,000	total £300,000
many gifts @ £1,000–£4,999	total £150,000

Three potential lead gifts totalling £4,500,000 represent 45% of the fundraising goal (the top gift alone represents 25%). Nearly forty gifts ranging from £50,000 to £500,000 would yield just over another 45%, and the balance could comprise hundreds of gifts between £1,000 and £10,000. This campaign envisages a modest number of gifts of relatively high value.

But the campaign could be structured another way.

Sample gift table 2	
2 gifts @ £1,500,000	total £3,000,000
1 gift @ £1,000,000	total £1,000,000
4 gifts @ £500,000	total £2,000,000
5 gifts @ £200,000	total £1,000,000
6 gifts @ £100,000	total £600,000
10 gifts @ £50,000	total £500,000
16 gifts @ £25,000	total £400,000
40 gifts @ £10,000	total £400,000
100 gifts @ £5,000	total £500,000
many, many gifts @ £100–£4,999	total £600,000

This gift table moves the weight of the campaign to lower levels of giving. Three lead gifts yield 40% of the total, but then the burden shifts to a larger number of donors giving smaller amounts. Note that the bottom level, with thousands of gifts ranging from only £100 to £4,999, suggests a broad 'grassroots' or alumni fundraising effort. Nonetheless, the percentages are close to the earlier model. The middle ground, gifts from £25,000 to £500,000, represents 45% of the total, and the lowest levels fill up the remaining 15%.

This is not a scientific process. It is simply a way to help you gauge whether you have the right mix of donors to make certain that you can reach your goal within a reasonable period of time.

Try drawing several gift tables to meet your fundraising goal. Using the assessments of funding potential described earlier in this chapter, slot your projections in at the appropriate gift levels. Experiment with different mixes; see if you can discern the likely 'shape' of your campaign. Begin with the highest lead gifts that you can identify with reasonable confidence (don't forget to include projections for a National Lottery bid or other major government funding). As you work your way down the table, be cautious: remember that some gifts will fall short of your projections, that some of your most loyal donors may disappoint you, and that it may require multiple requests to achieve a single gift of a given size.

As with the other resource assessment exercises discussed in this chapter, gift tables can show you what work needs to be done. You may not be able to identify enough lead gifts to launch your campaign right away. You may recognise the need for more board capacity to make and ask for large gifts. You may not have enough prospects to fill each gift level; your table will tell you where you need to target your efforts, or possibly tell you that you can make the goal by focusing on a few gift levels where you have the greatest strength and potential. This information in turn will help you plan the fundraising strategies and timetable of your campaign (see Chapter 9).

Building organisational capacity

Now we will consider other organisational resources necessary to run an effective and efficient campaign. Good leadership and generous donors are critical to the success of a campaign, but these assets can be squandered if you do not know how to manage them properly.

Fundraising skills

It is rare for an organisation to run a capital campaign without expanding its fundraising staff. However, skills are more important than quantity.

Just as you made a dispassionate assessment of your board leadership, you must make a dispassionate assessment of your fundraising staff. This is the time to assure that everyone in your development office is equal to the challenge that a campaign will bring. You need people with energy, people who have mastered the nuts and bolts of fundraising, people who can handle heavy workloads efficiently, people who can function under pressure, people who can speak and write clearly, and if possible, at least some people in senior positions who have campaign experience. You need to replace people who are not up to the job.

Your donor and prospect charts and gift tables can tell you more about the specific skills you should look for. If you expect to be preparing a National Lottery application, you need someone who knows how to go about it. If you are seeking multiple corporate sponsorships, which can involve complex and sometimes very technical negotiation, you want someone with relevant experience. Legacy fundraising is another area that requires technical expertise. Trust applications require good analytical and writing skills. Your board members, top individual donors and prospects and your fundraising volunteers should be tended by staff with major gifts experience. You will probably want an able researcher to help identify new prospects.

There is no magic formula to tell you how many fundraising staff you should have. To avoid overstaffing in certain areas and understaffing in others, wait until your needs are clearly delineated and expand slowly, with the emphasis on quality. Capital campaigns often stir up organisational resentment as other staff see substantial resources targeted to fundraising, but the process of campaign planning itself should make the case that professional fundraising capability is a necessity.

Communications and marketing

Your campaign will be played out on a public stage. It will draw energy from the excitement and 'buzz' that you create around it – even before it begins (see Chapter 7).

You need staff with professional experience in press and media relations and other forms of publicity. (Even if you use an independent public relations consultant, you may want some in-house staff to attend to day-to-day business.) If your strategic and campaign plans call for increased earned revenue to help reach your goals, you will have to expand your marketing capacity. Review your plans, and try to define the additional communications and marketing resources you will need.

Events

A capital campaign generates events of all kinds. There will be dinners, garden parties, receptions, performances, and tours to cultivate donors and to thank them. There will public events (shaped by your press strategy) to launch the campaign, to dig the first hole for a new building, to open a new building, and to introduce your new programme initiatives. You may give benefit events as fundraisers.

Planning and executing events is a skill all on its own. Whether you use a consultant or hire events staff, you will need this skill as a resource throughout the campaign.

(And, by the way, all fundraising, communications, and other staff whose jobs are directly related to the campaign must be on notice that they are expected to help out at campaign events, which often require many pairs of hands to run smoothly.)

Finance

Accurate, efficient budgeting and accounting are essential to a campaign. Without them, you won't know how much money you need and you won't be able to keep track of the money you have.

As campaign planning proceeds, you will need increasingly detailed budgets for each component of your goals. Accurate budgeting corroborates the case for your goals. Both finance and fundraising staff must understand the meaning of every line of every budget. By the time your fundraising begins you should have sufficient command of the budgets for each project to be able to present them in different ways to meet the interests and requirements of different donors.

Campaign fundraising will complicate your accounting tasks. You must be able to track every pound and penny that comes through the door: in the aggregate, project by project, and often grant by grant. Your yearly financial statements must be clear and precise. You will need to produce reports for your donors to account for the expenditure of their gifts and grants. To enable your trustees to monitor the campaign, you will need to produce periodic reports showing progress toward each of your goals, and from time to time you will release some of this information to the public.

If your campaign includes an endowment goal, you will need staff with experience in managing investments.

Examine your budgeting, accounting and financial management capabilities. You may decide to enlarge your staff, but more importantly, you must be confident of its competence.

Information management

Fundraising is fuelled by information. A capital campaign produces astonishing amounts of information. You will make lists of donors, lists of prospects, lists of people who are invited to events and people who come to events, lists of people who receive annual reports and campaign publications, lists of people who know other people. You will keep records of all gifts and grants, and thick files with donor histories and donor and prospect research. You will make diaries of visits and telephone calls and contacts with donors and prospects, and 'tickler' files to remind you when it is time to make future contact. You will make lists of proposal and report deadlines. You will track budgets and revenues and expenditures.

You are probably already drowning in all these types of information; a campaign will simply increase the load. If information is to be an asset and not a hindrance, you need to manage it well.

It may be tempting to purchase one of the many purpose-built fundraising and donor record management systems on the market. Proceed carefully: these can be expensive, they do not always perform as advertised, they are not always compatible with accounting systems, and the process of conversion to a new system can be tortuous. It might make sense for a large or rapidly growing organisation to make the investment. But it is not essential: a smaller organisation can function just as well with the spreadsheets and databases that come as standard applications on everyday computers. The key is not the sophistication of your technology: it is the quality of your information management practices.

Pay attention to this issue from the beginning of your campaign planning process. Designate a person or persons to guide the formulation of clear, consistent information management policies and to supervise compliance within and across organisational departments. Whatever technology you choose, make certain there is always someone on your staff who understands it and can troubleshoot when something goes awry. Remember that some of the information you collect will be confidential, and if mishandled, a violation of someone's privacy; you have both legal and ethical obligations to protect it. Make certain everyone understands that good information management is essential for a well-run campaign.

Paying for the campaign

Another axiom of fundraising is that it costs money to raise money. How will you pay for a capital campaign?

When your organisation makes the decision to undertake a campaign, it acknowledges the need to invest in the necessary resources. Most recurring costs, like fundraising and communications staff, publications, donor stewardship, and events, will have to be built into your annual operating budgets for the period of the campaign. But you may be able to find supplementary funding for some one-off costs, such as strategic planning, a feasibility study (see Chapter 5), the planning of a new programme initiative, or the design phase of a new building. For example, some charitable trusts will make grants for purposes like these 'to strengthen organisational capacity'. It is not uncommon for a board member or a long-time major individual donor to underwrite some of the expenditures leading up to a capital campaign.

Campaign costs are not 'extras': they are an investment in the organisation's future, and if the campaign is successful, the return on investment will be substantial.

CHAPTER FIVE
Getting ready: testing your assumptions

You have developed the rationale for a capital campaign, set goals, and conducted a resource assessment to test whether you can meet your goals. It's beginning to look like a real campaign plan, and you think you are ready to go. But before you make a final decision, you should take one more step to test your assumptions with a feasibility study. This is an exercise that allows your friends to let you know whether they think you have a winning case.

Feasibility studies: what they tell you and why they matter

A feasibility study, sometimes called a readiness assessment or a campaign planning study, asks your trustees, major donors, major prospects, and community opinion leaders to express their candid opinions of your organisation, campaign goals, and fundraising plan in a series of confidential interviews conducted by an independent third party. The responses are delivered in a report that shields them from attribution, and that indicates how you can strengthen or rethink aspects of your plan to improve your chances of success. The 'independent third party' is usually a consultant, which means that a feasibility study costs money.

Is a feasibility study mandatory? No, but in most instances it is advisable. If your resource assessment leaves you feeling elated with confidence, if you are absolutely certain that you have everything you need for a successful campaign, perhaps you are ready to move ahead immediately. Otherwise, the investment in a feasibility study could save you from making serious mistakes. No one relishes criticism, but it is better to hear it now than later, when the campaign is well under way. The results of a feasibility study may lead you to address potentially serious organisational problems, reconsider some aspects of your fundraising plan, reconsider the way you present your case, reconsider your campaign goals and timetable – and in rare cases, alert you to the reality that you are not quite ready for a capital campaign.

The feasibility study serves your campaign in other ways as well. It is an opportunity to build and strengthen your relationships with the very people on whom your campaign will rely most heavily: your board, major donors and prospects (not just individuals, but trusts and companies as well), and community leaders. It is a very important step in the cultivation process for lead gifts, and it is your first opportunity to float your campaign message to a wider audience.

How to do a feasibility study

The key to a constructive feasibility study is candour: the key to candour is confidentiality. No one wants to be seen as a naysayer. Some of your trustees, including those who have been actively involved in strategic and campaign planning, may have concerns they are loath to express publicly or even privately to other trustees or staff members. The same may be true of donors and prospects and community leaders who value your work and may have close personal connections within the organisation. That is why you need an independent consultant to do your study.

Your consultant is by definition an outsider, and therefore will have to spend considerable time learning about your organisation, its mission, its goals, and the reasoning behind its campaign plan. All the planning exercises and worksheets you have completed thus far should be shared with your consultant, and they should work closely with your board chair, chief executive and fundraising staff to identify the people to be interviewed and to craft interview questions. A large, complex organisation, like a university, might compile a list of as many as 75 to 100 potential interviewees; a smaller organisation might be able to identify only 10 to 15 candidates at most. The list should always include your trustees, even those who, at this stage, seem unlikely to play an active part in the campaign.

The consultant will develop an interview questionnaire that elicits comments on issues like the following.

• The respondent's overall impressions of the organisation, its mission, its effectiveness, the value of its activities and services.

• Impressions of the chair and chief executive.

• Impressions of the board's effectiveness as a governing body, and as the source of leadership in a campaign.

• The merits of the purposes and projects set forth in the campaign plan, and the likelihood that those purposes can be achieved and sustained.

• How well the organisation has expressed the case for the campaign.

• Perceptions of the strength of the organisation's donor base and prospect pool, the feasibility of the proposed gift table, and the organisation's ability to meet its fundraising goals.

- An indication of the respondent's own interest in participating in the campaign: the possibility that they would consider substantial financial support or work as a volunteer in campaign activities or both.

You have to make a few preparations to conduct these feasibility interviews. You will need to polish up the draft of your case statement (see Chapter 3) into a few attractively presented pages. Word processing is enough; this is not yet the time for a published brochure. Keep it brief – three to four pages. Try to avoid overheated rhetoric, and let the reader follow a clear progression from the logic of your strategic plan to your case for a campaign. Append concise descriptions of the component campaign goals (buildings, new programme initiatives, new projects, endowment, operations). If you have preliminary drawings of a new building or other simple illustrative material, append these also. A reader should be able to glance through the entire package in fifteen minutes.

An introductory letter should be sent to all potential interviewees, signed by the chief executive or board chair or, preferably, both. It should explain that your organisation has reached an important crossroads in assessing its accomplishments and determining its future direction, that you are planning a capital campaign, and that you would value their participation in the planning process. Let them know that consultant X will soon be contacting them to schedule a personal interview; it will be strictly confidential and take no longer than one hour. Assure them that they will not be asked for a gift or any other commitment at this meeting. Enclose your draft case statement and other materials described earlier.

Prepare a clean version of your gift table, showing the number of gifts (but not the identity of the prospects) that you project at each level to achieve 100% of your goal. This should not be sent in advance; the consultant will show it to interviewees in the course of the conversation, ask if they think it is feasible based on what they know of the organisation's circle of support, and possibly ask what level of giving they might consider if approached at the appropriate time.

Immediately after each interview, a thank-you letter should be sent by the chief executive or chair.

When all the interviews are completed, the consultant will prepare a detailed report. This is not a statistical analysis of the responses; the sample in most feasibility studies is too small to be statistically valid, and in any event the responses of interviewees have to be weighted in accordance with their importance to the organisation. You will not be given the raw interview data, but the consultant will pass along certain information, such as the size of potential gifts from specific respondents or their willingness to help with campaign activities, that require follow-up action on your part.

How to interpret a feasibility study

The consultant's report will contain conclusions and recommendations on the issues described above, and on any other issues that come up in the interviews that could be pertinent to your campaign. It will reflect the opinions of people who sincerely care about the organisation and its future, but who may have reservations and concerns or who may look at things from a completely different perspective, and it will give you a sense of their likely intentions to participate in the campaign.

Here are some of the clues you should look for in your feasibility report.

• Your potential lead donors may be sceptical that your donor pool is sufficient to reach your fundraising goals, and therefore reluctant to commit to large gifts until they are confident that the goals can be achieved.

• You may not have made the most persuasive case for the purposes of the campaign. For example, have you simply asserted the artistic arguments for a new theatre, or have you also demonstrated how it will increase your audience and be more economical to run than continuing your reliance upon rented performance and rehearsal space? Your case must be broad enough to answer the viewpoints, and possibly the prejudices, of a variety of readers.

• There may be doubts that you can sustain the new assets you plan to create. Have you sufficiently addressed this concern?

• Perceptions of your organisation among opinion leaders in the community may be different from what you expected. You will want to think how to capitalise on the positive and counteract the negative.

• Organisational issues may be perceived as potentially harmful to the campaign; for example, weak administrative capacity, a common problem in organisations founded and directed by a single charismatic leader.

• You should be able to get a sense of your board's enthusiasm, commitment, and willingness to pitch in and work for the campaign, even if they have some reservations.

Consider what you have learned from your feasibility study and how you can apply these lessons. The fact that some respondents may hesitate or disagree does not necessarily mean that they are right, but their perceptions may influence their willingness to support your campaign and therefore should be addressed. Only in rare instances will a feasibility study tell you that a campaign is impossible; almost always, it will tell you how to make a better plan.

Back to the drawing board

At several points in preceding chapters you have been advised to stop, delay, and reconsider. With the completion of your feasibility study, you have come to the point of decision: whether to launch a capital campaign, and if so, what the campaign should look like.

By now, if you have followed a thorough planning process, you will have accounted for all contingencies you can reasonably be expected to foresee, and you will be well prepared to exploit the opportunities and overcome the obstacles that lie before you. Go back to the drawing board one more time and, in light of all you have learned, consider the following issues.

Are you ready for a capital campaign? The final review

• Revisit your goals. Are there certain components that don't fit well within the overall campaign scope or seem unlikely to attract support, and that might be set aside for action at a later time? Do you need to scale down your aspirations to a more realistic level?

• Revisit your fundraising goals. Are you reasonably confident you can raise not only the total goal, but also the goals established for each component of the campaign? Are you confident that you can maintain your operating base throughout the campaign, and subsequently sustain a higher operating base to support your new capital assets? Do you need to reduce your reliance on fundraising and look to alternative sources of financial support, such as increased earned income? Or, have you discovered that your fundraising potential is actually greater than you suspected? This might mean that you can expand your campaign scope and goals!

• Revisit your leadership. Is your board strong enough to carry its leadership responsibilities through the challenges of a campaign? Will your board members contribute financially, and will they work?

• Revisit your organisational capacity to manage a campaign. Do you know where you need to strengthen your capacity, and do you have a plan and the resources to do it?

• Revisit your timetable. Are you ready to start the campaign right away or do you have more preparatory work to complete? Should you stretch the duration of the campaign over a greater number of years; conversely, could you reach your goals more quickly than you originally thought? Should you consider launching a 'mini-campaign' for your single most urgent need first, and fold in other needs once you have established a strong momentum?

● Revisit your case statement. Will your arguments be persuasive not only to insiders, but to the wider community and the general public?

When you have addressed all these questions to the best of your ability and amended your plan accordingly, it is time to present the final plan to your board of trustees for approval. And now you are on your way!

CHAPTER SIX

Components of a capital campaign: organising leadership

The identification and assessment of leadership as a fundraising resource was an important element in your planning process. Presumably, having come this far, you feel confident that you have sufficient leadership potential to carry your campaign forward, but that potential cannot be fully realised unless it is properly organised and well supported. This chapter will discuss some of the leadership structures and support systems frequently used in capital campaigns, and describe some basic principles of leadership support that can be adapted to your particular needs.

Take a quick look back at the enumeration of board fundraising responsibilities in Chapter 4. The responsibilities of campaign leadership are essentially the same. Trustees will constitute the core of your campaign leadership and (one hopes) your most active fundraising volunteers, but you will also want to enlist other volunteers with exceptional skills, commitment, and standing in the community. Some of these may be major donors; others, people who have played a prominent role in the life of the organisation in some other way.

Campaign leadership is not static. As the campaign progresses, you will be able to motivate additional board members and other volunteers to work on behalf of a winning enterprise.

Leadership structures

The central organising structure for campaign leadership is the campaign committee, sometimes called the campaign steering committee. This is a working committee, not an honorary body. Most but not all of its members will be trustees, and it should be chaired by a trustee who has some knowledge and experience of fundraising. Perhaps your organisation already has a development committee; the campaign committee could evolve from the membership of this group, with a few changes and additions that would serve the needs of your capital campaign. Look for people who have social, community, and business networks and the willingness to use them, for people who can speak eloquently about the organisation's mission, and for people who can work smoothly with colleagues and staff in a team effort.

It is customary for the board chair to be a member of the campaign committee, but not necessarily the committee chair. Assigning this position to a different trustee allows you to exploit the talents of another gifted leader, and acknowledges the reality that the board chair has other responsibilities to carry in addition to the burdens of a campaign. If you are lucky enough to have several outstanding candidates, you might consider a committee headed by two equal co-chairs.

Once you have identified the most promising trustees for your campaign committee, look at a wider circle of major donors and volunteers. They can bring a refreshing independent perspective and new contacts and networks to enlarge your prospect pool. But do not shift the centre of gravity too far away from the board. You do not want to dilute your board's sense of collective responsibility for the campaign, nor its duty to preserve the integrity of the organisation's mission and values under the stress of intensive campaign fundraising.

How large should your campaign committee be? In a small organisation it might have only four or five members; in a large organisation, perhaps as many as fifteen. The important thing is that all committee members must be capable and willing to work actively on campaign fundraising.

Some capital campaigns also set up sub-committees that focus on specific fundraising goals. For example, at a university where the establishment of a theatre department is a major campaign goal, a special sub-committee might be appointed to concentrate on fundraising from sources specifically interested in theatre arts. In many large campaigns it is common to have an annual fund sub-committee, which focuses on cultivating donors for the critical operating base. These sub-committees also consist of a mix of trustees and non-trustee volunteers, and maintain a liaison to the board either directly or through the campaign committee.

A question sometimes arises about the appointment of celebrities to campaign committees, for instance, a famous actor for a theatre company, or an eminent public figure for a charity working to end world hunger. If the purpose is simply to reap the public relations benefits of name recognition, there are better ways. One often-used strategy is to set up an 'advisory council' or 'honorary board' of distinguished names. Its members might be called upon to endorse the campaign and to participate from time to time in various campaign activities (signing letters, appearing at events, etc.), and their association with the campaign signals their public commitment to the organisation and its goals. But the leadership structures we are discussing here are true working bodies. They will meet regularly, and in between meetings their members will be assigned specific tasks and obligations. Choose people who can make the time and the commitment to take on these obligations.

The campaign committee at work

If you have reread the overview of board responsibilities for fundraising in Chapter 4, this discussion of campaign committee responsibilities will look familiar. In collaboration with the chief executive and fundraising staff, the committee and its various sub-committees work to expand the organisation's donor base and increase giving by donors at all levels.

As a precondition, committee members must themselves be contributors to the campaign, commensurate with their ability to give. The degree to which they have stretched to support extraordinary organisational needs and aspirations will provide the standard and the inspiration for other donors to follow. Remember the principle of proportionality. The amount of a gift is not as important as the relationship of that amount to the donor's ability to give. Once they have made their own contributions, committee members are empowered to ask others to do the same.

Committee members will put significant time into 'prospecting', answering the query who do you know and what do you know about them? They will comb their own networks to suggest new prospects (individuals, trusts, and companies) for further staff research; review lists of prospects compiled by staff to see if they can identify personal contacts or suggest other people who might have personal contacts; and consider whether current donors whom they know can be persuaded to increase their level of giving. Some of this work is done in groups at committee meetings, but much can be accomplished in one-on-one meetings with staff. The committee's prospecting work begins when the campaign begins and continues to its end, in ever-widening ripples into a broader prospect pool.

An outgrowth of prospecting is cultivation. As new prospects and major donors are assessed, committee members will be asked to open doors to people they know: write introductory letters or make telephone calls; encourage prospects to visit the organisation, meet with programme staff, and see its work in progress; invite prospects as their personal guests to receptions, performances and special campaign events. After each prospect review every committee member should leave with a list of assigned cultivation tasks.

Following on from donor cultivation, campaign committee members are expected to ask for gifts: by signing request letters and proposals, in private face-to-face meetings with prospects, and at campaign events. Decisions about who asks whom will be made in discussions between committee members and staff, and the timing, content, and format of each request will be carefully planned.

Finally, you will rely on committee members to nurture relationships with donors they know by participating in stewardship activities: signing thank-you letters and making thank-you telephone calls immediately after gifts are received; inviting donors to events; hosting an occasional private luncheon or visit 'behind the scenes' so that donors can see how their gifts have been put to good use. The purpose, of course, is to keep donors close to the organisation through a personal connection that may lead to repeated and increased support.

In addition to its direct participation in fundraising, the campaign committee can reach out to other board members and potential volunteers to become involved as well. The objective is to spread the committee's own enthusiasm and, by example, to demonstrate that one person's actions can make a tangible difference – and that success can be exhilarating!

The campaign committee will monitor the progress of the campaign and report periodically to the board. Every board meeting should reserve substantial time for a campaign report that highlights important accomplishments, notes areas that need more work, and reinforces the need for the participation of every board member in a collective and challenging enterprise.

Support: the key to volunteer success

Your fundraising volunteers, including your hardworking trustees, live real lives that have nothing to do with your campaign; they have families, demanding jobs, and other important community obligations. How on earth can they be expected to take upon themselves all the tasks we have just described? Apart from the prodigious commitment of time, where will they get the skills, the confidence, and in some circumstances the sheer courage?

The answer is that they must be strongly supported by your chief executive and staff – not just fundraising staff, but all staff. In every instance, volunteers' obligations must be pared down to those actions that only they can undertake. You must do whatever is necessary to prepare for and follow up on their work.

Here are some of the ways in which you can (indeed, must) support your board, campaign committee, and other fundraising volunteers.

Support for fundraising volunteers

● In preparation for all discussions of prospecting and cultivation, you must provide comprehensive, accurate background research, succinctly presented on the prospect's interests, assets and giving potential, community and philanthropic commitments, contacts and networks. Your committee members may be able to fill in the gaps and provide additional bits of information from personal knowledge, but they should not be expected to supply information that you can obtain through your own research efforts.

• It is unreasonable to expect volunteers, even trustees who have been associated with the organisation for a long time, to be able to speak extemporaneously about the organisation generally or the campaign in particular. They need access to information in an easily retrievable and readable form. Pocket-sized 'cheat sheets' with basic facts about the organisation and the goals of the campaign are one useful device to fill this need.

• Fundraising volunteers must be fully briefed in advance for any personal contact with a prospect or donor, even one whom they know well. They must have full background information on the prospect to prevent any avoidable misstep or embarrassment. They must know enough about the subject matter for discussion (a specific campaign goal or project, for example) to be able to speak with conviction. A staff presence, including staff working directly on the specific project or activities under discussion, is necessary in any personal meeting with a prospect or donor that will delve deeply into content. The volunteer is the bearer of the 'message' but is not an expert on content.

• Staff should prepare drafts of letters that volunteers will sign. It is quicker and easier for a volunteer to edit or rewrite a draft than to sit down in front of a blank sheet of paper. Drafts of thank-you letters for gifts received are especially important, since these are time-sensitive.

• Staff should prepare suggested 'talking points' for all telephone calls and meetings, and these should be reviewed with fundraising volunteers in advance. The talking points should be backed up by factual information on issues that might come up in the course of the conversation.

• Rehearse in advance for any conversation with a prospect who might raise difficult questions or objections, or who might refuse your appeal on the spot. Rejection is difficult enough for professional fundraising staff to deal with, but more so for a volunteer. Volunteers need to build confidence, by understanding that even an apparent rejection may lead to more positive results in the future.

• Give your fundraising volunteers some basic information on donors and prospects they might encounter at campaign events, so that they can react appropriately. 'Thank you, Mr G, for your generous gift' is enough, but even this simple sentence requires the knowledge that Mr G will be present and that he has made a substantial gift.

• Fundraising volunteers must know who they can call in the organisation to get help or answer questions, often at short notice. All staff, not just fundraising staff, must be alert to the needs of fundraising volunteers for support.

● Give your fundraising volunteers an 'exit strategy': in other words, don't allow them to feel that their commitment is endless. Discuss and assign a few tasks at a time, and make certain that these tasks have been carried through to mutual satisfaction, before compiling the next list. If your volunteers feel proud of work well done so far, they will be ready to take on more.

● Above all, make certain that your fundraising volunteers receive lavish credit – both publicly and privately expressed – for the success of their efforts. We all know that behind every successful volunteer lies a great deal of painstaking staff support. But this is the way it should be. Your organisation will profit if it is publicly perceived to have an active, productive, committed cadre of fundraising volunteers.

CHAPTER SEVEN

Components of a capital campaign: how will you tell the story?

Every successful capital campaign grows out of a compelling story. This chapter will discuss how to tell your story. It is not a lesson in public relations, simply a checklist of the kinds of strategies and materials you will need to tell your story effectively, at the right time, and to the right audience.

Setting the stage

How can you expect people to dig deep into their pockets to support an organisation they've barely heard of? You can't.

Long before you start your campaign, even before you have a campaign plan, you need to make your organisation visible. At the first moment you suspect that a capital campaign may be in your future, take steps to increase public awareness of who you are, what you do, and why you matter. Try to get more media coverage of your work. Market your website more aggressively, and use it to present timely feature stories on interesting projects and activities. Publish your newsletter more frequently. Plan events that will allow members of the public to see your organisation at work.

It will take many months, perhaps several years, of preparation before you are ready to publicise your plans for organisational growth or announce a campaign. Use this time well to foster your image as an important, dynamic organisation worthy of public attention and support. Increasing your visibility over a long lead time in advance of a campaign will increase your chances of success.

The case statement

Just as a synopsis summarises the story line of a play, the case statement summarises the story line of your campaign.

Your case statement grows directly out of the mission, values, vision, challenges, and priorities defined in your strategic plan. It started life as a brief rough draft in the early stages of campaign planning (see Chapter 3), and re-emerged in more polished but still preliminary form as part of your feasibility study (see Chapter 5). As soon as you decide that you will have a capital campaign, it is time to prepare a complete case statement.

A case statement is an attractive presentational publication, usually peppered with lots of photographs and illustrations. Couched in robust, confident language, it sets out the organisation's mission, its proudest accomplishments and strengths, an inspirational vision for the future, and the goals of the capital campaign. In format, case statements may range from professionally designed four-colour soft-cover books on glossy paper, to more modest efforts produced on desktop computers. The case statement is presented privately to lead gift donors and prospects in the earliest culti-vation stages of the campaign, and distributed to a wider public when the campaign is formally announced.

The preparation of a case statement represents a substantial invest-ment of time and money. It may be useful to consider some of the most frequent pitfalls that organisations encounter in the development of their case statements.

Case statement alerts

● Case statements age quickly. Many are obsolete within months of their publication. This is because case statements often describe the organisation and the campaign frozen at a particular moment in time. But time moves on, and both internally and externally the context for the campaign changes subtly but noticeably. Focus your narrative on the broad themes; avoid references and factual details that will date your text. It may help to adopt a flexible format, perhaps a pocket in the back cover where up-to-date descriptions of the campaign goals and reports of campaign progress can be inserted.

● You will find the task of writing a case statement very difficult if you have skipped the earlier phases of development described in Chapters 3 and 5. But if you have already made your way through several drafts, as part of your campaign planning and again for your feasibility study, many of the thorniest problems will be resolved by the time you set to work on the final, formal publication.

● Many organisations spend far too much money on case statements. It is understandable that you will want a handsome publication, with good photography and illustration, bright colours and a vibrant design. But remember that the case statement, though it is crucially important, has limited uses. Later in the campaign you will need other kinds of publications to reach different, wider audiences. Don't deplete your publications budget, and your energy, in a quest for the ideal campaign case statement.

Telling all your stories

You will tell the story of your campaign to many audiences. Some will want to hear about the whole campaign; others will be interested only in one of its component goals. Think ahead to the kinds of materials you might need to develop for all the audiences you intend to reach.

Modern computer technology has made it possible to produce text, graphics, images, and even sound in interchangeable formats. We can recycle many of the same source materials to develop printed publications, large-scale renderings, slide shows, and multi-media presentations that can be seen up close on a laptop or projected to a screen in a large auditorium. If you use it prudently, resisting the temptations and the risks of the 'cutting edge', this technology can give you a great degree of flexibility at reasonable cost.

One of the first items you are likely to need is a campaign overview, initially for the board, then for submission to your lead gift prospects, and eventually for your campaign announcement and other public forums such as meetings with community groups. For these occasions you may find it useful to supplement oral presentations with a media presentation of your case statement, distributing the printed case statement to your audience as a 'takeaway' document.

In a capital campaign for a building, you will probably produce a succession of presentations over time. Here, your architects can help; many are quite savvy about the fundraising and marketing aspects of construction projects. At the very beginning you will need drawings of your general design concept (both external and internal) even if these change, as they often do, as the work progresses. Later you may be able to produce more detailed cutaway views, computer renderings of specific spaces, and even virtual tours of the building. All of these will be useful to cultivate lead gifts, allow donors to visualise potential naming opportunities, and achieve community support.

You may design 'mini-campaigns' targeted at particular audiences. For example, one of your strategies for increasing operating support might be an appeal directly to your membership, perhaps challenging them to reach a specified goal. For this purpose you will need a special publication, essentially a mini-case statement (perhaps in the form of a brochure) that can be distributed widely by direct mail and at cultivation events.

You will be making dozens, perhaps hundreds, of presentations to individuals, trusts, government funders, and companies, cultivating their support for the campaign projects that are most relevant to their interests. Most of these will require an individualised set of presentation materials. However, you can lay the groundwork in advance by preparing summary narratives for each project, along with fact sheets and illustrations – all in formats that are easily kept up to date. These can be assembled as needed into attractive presentation packets for use in face-to-face meetings and to leave behind for the prospect to reread later. For major projects you may also want to have a laptop presentation that can be shown in meetings with donors and prospects.

Don't forget that many of your audiences will know very little about your organisation. Prepare basic information packets that clearly describe your mission, your history, the scope of your activities, your major accomplishments, your annual operating budget, a list of your trustees, and anything else you think could help people get to know you.

Don't forget materials for the media. Your public relations experts can tell you what they will need to brief the press, from the moment you announce your campaign through every newsworthy event, such as an unusually large gift or groundbreaking for a building, until your goal is finally achieved.

And don't forget your website. It is a wonderful vehicle for reaching an audience that has no geographical limits. Keep it fresh, attractive, and up to date.

Finally, there is the story of the campaign itself. Some organisations send out occasional newsletters to their donors with feature stories on large gifts, listings of donors to date, and reports on progress toward the campaign goals. Most publish a summary report at the end of the campaign, celebrating its achievements and thanking its donors. These publications are essentially addressed to donors rather than to the general public; they may not be necessary in every case, but they can serve an important stewardship function.

Given the intensity and fast pace of fundraising in a capital campaign, you can never entirely avoid the last-minute scramble to pull something together for a meeting or event. But with some advance planning you can prepare (and budget for) the basic tools to broadcast your story widely, and with force and flair.

CHAPTER EIGHT

Components of a capital campaign: donor recognition and stewardship

Donor recognition is the public acknowledgement of philanthropic support. Stewardship has been characterised, somewhat impishly, as the 'care and feeding of donors'. Donor recognition and stewardship are essential elements in building the relationships that will secure the goals of your campaign and lay the foundation for continuing, growing support in the future.

Donor stewardship is part of the art and craft of fundraising, a subject broad enough to fill a volume in itself (see the *Further Reading* section at the end of this book). This chapter will address the most important aspects of donor recognition and stewardship that need to be factored into a capital campaign plan. Specifically, we will look at issues that should be resolved well before you begin fundraising. In this area, as in some others discussed earlier, improvisation can lead to chaos.

Donor recognition: naming opportunities

Donors' motivations for giving are numerous and complex. One among these is the desire for public acknowledgement, perhaps as a symbol of (or a way to achieve) status in the community, perhaps because public visibility furthers other objectives (such as a company's desire for name recognition as an element of its own marketing strategy), perhaps out of a simple human desire to have one's good deeds noticed and appreciated.

Naming a space or a building, a charitable endowment, or an institution after a donor has an honourable history; it is certainly the most enduring form of donor recognition, dating back at least as far as medieval times. A capital campaign provides many possibilities for naming opportunities because you are creating permanent capital assets that can commemorate a donor's name far into the future.

As you plan the naming opportunities for your campaign, here are a few issues that you need to bear in mind.

• Your outline of naming opportunities should be established before the campaign begins. Both you and your prospective donors must be clear on the conditions attached to each naming opportunity, to avoid later misunderstandings or resentments.

• Consider setting some of the most desirable naming opportunities slightly higher than the expectations reflected on your gift table, so that donors are motivated to stretch to reach the prize.

• Remember that donors' names will be permanently attached to your assets, thus precluding naming opportunities for larger gifts that may come along later. Therefore, try to define naming opportunities in a way that leaves room for your future fundraising needs. (What happens, for example, when your new building requires a complete refurbishment in twenty years' time? What kind of donor recognition will your successors be able to offer donors in a future capital campaign?)

• Don't lose sight of the fact that there are many attractive alternative means to offer donor recognition and visibility other than a permanent naming opportunity. These will be discussed in a later section of this chapter.

Buildings and spaces

Buildings and their interior spaces are the classic naming opportunities in a capital campaign, and the 'jewels in the crown' for the recognition of lead gifts.

As the first step in devising your naming opportunity plan, you need to identify all the potential building components that could be suitable for naming. Many, such as the building itself, separate building wings, foyers and lobbies, outdoor plazas, reading rooms, galleries and auditoriums, are obvious. But less publicly visible spaces may also be appealing to certain donors. For instance, even in a building that will be used primarily for offices and client services, there may be meeting and conference rooms or a suite of rooms where staff meet privately with clients that could be meaningful naming opportunities for some donors.

As soon as you have a reasonably complete (though not necessarily final) design for your building and an estimate of your campaign fundraising goals, you can begin sketching a naming opportunity table. Opportunities are graded according to levels of giving, and these are defined in relationship to your total fundraising goal. Remember that you are seeking lead gifts for the entire scope of your campaign, and accordingly, attach naming opportunities to gifts that may encompass a range of related campaign needs, not just construction costs. For example, if you have set £7,000,000 as the requirement for naming an auditorium, the gift might include some money toward construction, some for current operating support, and some toward an endowment to support the future operating costs of activities within the auditorium. This is another reason to set a relatively high 'price' for each naming opportunity, since qualifying gifts must move you significantly forward toward your overall campaign goal, not just your construction budget.

It is worth reiterating the point made earlier: naming opportunities in buildings are permanent, and may constrict your future options for fundraising or for making changes in the building itself. Use this form of donor recognition sparingly, and try to negotiate agreements with your donors that leave sufficient flexibility to meet future needs. It is, after all, in the donor's own interest to assure that a building or space that perpetuates the donor's name and memory will be well maintained and capable of serving the organisation's needs for decades to come.

A related point, often forgotten, is what happens when you have to demolish an existing named building or space to make way for a new one. How can you continue to honour the name of the original donor while recognising the new one? (One possibility is a commemorative plaque mounted prominently within the new building.) Even if your current donors and prospects are eager to take centre stage, they will appreciate the need for sensitivity on this issue, since their own names could easily be superseded in the same way in the future.

Your naming opportunity scheme will not be final until you have an approved building design, an agreed set of campaign fundraising goals, and a gift table that has, if possible, been tested in a feasibility study. The first draft of a naming opportunity table for a capital campaign to build and endow a new theatre might look something like the following example.

Sample naming opportunity table for a building	
Naming opportunity	**Gift**
Theatre: building	£15,000,000
Main auditorium	£12,000,000
Small auditorium/rehearsal space	£10,000,000
Entrance foyer	£5,000,000
Small auditorium foyer	£3,000,000
VIP reception room	£2,000,000

Note that this hypothetical scheme is designed to reflect proportionality between the relative size of a gift and the size and prominence of the space to be named, and posits a £15,000,000 lead gift to name the theatre building itself. Fifteen million may well be far above the highest lead gift you can reasonably anticipate, or it just might be within reach, given sufficient cultivation of your principal lead gift prospects. Is the amount feasible, or should you reduce the required gift level to entice your highest-ranked prospect, or should you assume that this naming opportunity will not be taken up by any donor and will remain available for future donors? The same questions can be raised regarding each proposed gift level, and the answers are a matter of judgement, informed by your assessment of your fundraising potential. Many very successful capital campaigns for buildings actually end up using only a few of the possible naming opportunities. It would be a mistake to develop your donor recognition strategy with too much reliance on this one technique, and, as noted earlier, it can in fact be very useful to have attractive naming opportunities remaining for future fundraising purposes.

Endowments

Compared to the intricacies of naming opportunities for a new building, naming opportunities for endowments are straightforward. Simply set a minimum gift level as the qualification to attach a donor's name to the endowment, and then link this privilege to a variety of opportunities for visibility, for example, publication of a list of all named endowments in your annual reports, or on a wall plaque in a prominent location, or on brochures and publicity materials describing the programme or activity supported by the endowment. (The public acknowledgement of gifts is discussed further later in this chapter.)

A named endowment should be reserved for donors at a reasonably high level: £250,000, £500,000 or even £1,000,000, depending on the size of your endowment goal. Donors of gifts for endowment at lower levels can be honoured with other forms of acknowledgement.

Programme initiatives

We have referred throughout this book to capital campaigns that create permanent new assets for a major programme initiative – examples have included the formation of a new department at a university, or a charity's expansion of its programme of children's services into another city. These new assets are theoretically available as naming opportunities, but it is difficult if not impossible to parse them into segments like the spaces in a building. There is also the danger that permanently naming a new department or an entire programme for a founding donor could make it harder to raise substantial operating gifts for that programme in the future. One possibility to consider is to offer naming opportunities on a time-limited basis, for example, to acknowledge a large gift that fully supports a new programme initiative over a given period of time. This option is particularly useful for named sponsorships of major events, such as sports matches or concert series, over an agreed period of years covered by the donor's gift.

Naming opportunity table

When you have determined all the naming opportunities you are prepared to offer, make another table similar to the one illustrated earlier, and slot in all naming opportunities for new capital assets (buildings, endowment, and programme) at their appropriate gift levels in descending order. Because naming opportunities are limited to higher gift levels, naming tables are seldom disseminated widely, but are usually part of a package of materials used in the cultivation of lead gift and major gift prospects.

The example naming opportunity table below (this time without numbers) shows how you might set up a naming opportunity plan for a capital campaign.

Sample naming opportunity table for a building	
Naming opportunity	**Gift**
Community sports centre: building	£
Main arena	£
Children's gymnasium	£
Hospitality/VIP reception room	£
Spectators' boxes (each)	£
Named endowments (minimum)	£
Named annual sports series (4 years)	£
Named annual children's sports series (4 years)	£

Donor recognition: forms of public acknowledgement

There are myriad creative and effective ways, other than naming opportunities, to give your donors public acknowledgement and visibility. You are probably using many of them in your current fundraising work, and you can adapt them easily to your capital campaign.

It has been observed that capital campaigns seem to spawn virtual forests of donor plaques. And this is true, because they are such a flexible and therefore useful form of donor recognition. A handsome wall plaque acknowledging major gifts toward a building is a good way to give donors 'ownership' as an alternative to a permanent naming opportunity, and it allows you to offer visibility to many donors whose gifts are not large enough to qualify for a naming opportunity. A plaque for collective acknowledgement, displayed in the entry or other prominent location, might list all major donors to the building, or individual plaques at various spots throughout the building might link a single donor's generosity to a specific space. Similar plaques can be specially tailored to acknowledge gifts for named endowments, as well as major gifts for new programme initiatives and for operating support. Some campaigns memorialise all their major contributors this way, in categories arranged by the size of their gifts rather than the purpose. Some examples are given here.

The Centre for Research in Genetic Medicine was created with a generous gift from the George and Mary Grey Family Trust

Additional major support was provided by
The Ralph and Susan Blue Charitable Trust
The Samuel White Family
The Red Rose Corporation
and
Emily and Henry Black

The University acknowledges the generous support of the
Molly and Roland Green Endowment for this rare books reading room.
Dedicated November 2006.

Mama's Kitchen gratefully acknowledges the generous support of the following major donors to its Campaign to End Hunger in Our City 2003–2006

Benefactors	Sponsors	Patrons
ABC Trust	DEF Corporation	George G
Henry and Helen H	JJ Charitable Trust	Kenneth K
LMN Company Ltd	Orson and Olivia O	Patricia P
Q Electronics Corporation	Ralph and Rita R	Simon S
TUV Charitable Trust	WXY Corporation	Zack Z

And the many other loyal friends of Mama's Kitchen

If you expect to use this form of donor recognition (and few capital campaigns do not), you should make some basic decisions in advance. What kinds of plaques will you install, and where, and what gift levels will be required in order to be listed on a plaque? Your plan will serve as a framework to provide consistency, to help avoid 'plaque clutter', and to enable you to offer individual and collective acknowledgement plaques to your prospects as an important donor benefit.

Acknowledging your donors in publications and on your website is another excellent means of donor recognition. Such acknowledgements are very flexible: they can encompass all categories of donors, or focus on a single donor or programme. You can publish long lists of donors (usually segmented by gift levels) in annual reports and newsletters that track the progress of the campaign; you can acknowledge the generosity of specific donors on fliers or a segment of your website describing a particular aspect of your work. Published acknowledgements reach a wide audience, and they give you the opportunity to recognise gifts at much lower levels than is possible on a wall plaque.

All these forms of public acknowledgement (plaques, publications, websites) need to be organised before you start your campaign. Make another table, like the one illustrated earlier for naming opportunities, and sketch a plan for various forms of public acknowledgement tied to specified gift levels. Is your plan logical, consistent, and proportional? Will it appear logical, consistent, and proportional to your donors?

Negotiated donor recognition

One of the reasons you need to plan donor recognition in advance is that, in the heat of the campaign, you will deal with many donors who have special demands and requirements for recognition. If you start with a plan in hand you can, in most cases, defer to these demands within the framework you have devised, and in the rare instances where it is necessary, you will have justification for deciding that these demands are unacceptable and need to be negotiated.

Grants from charitable trusts and many government funding sources often come with requirements for specific credit lines; these are seldom problematic. Occasionally, an individual donor may have 'delusions of grandeur' and demand a form of recognition that you do not feel is appropriate. In these circumstances it is usually possible to find a creative solution that does not violate the principles of consistency and parity with other donors at the same level. Lead gifts frequently are negotiated with forms of donor recognition and other benefits that go beyond the terms provided in your original plan, but which can be justified within the overall logic of the plan.

The area most likely to raise difficult issues of donor recognition is with corporations and businesses, for whom public visibility to specific audiences, often reflecting the goals of their own marketing strategies, is a primary motivation for contributing to a capital campaign. One much debated issue is the use of corporate logos in publications and on signs; another is the public perception of a particular corporate name in juxtaposition with the charity's stated mission; another is the corporation's use of its support for a charity as part of its own advertising and marketing campaigns. These are serious questions, to which you need to frame answers that preserve your organisational integrity and yet retain your ability to attract appropriate corporate and business support. If you have identified the corporate sector as a significant segment of your campaign prospect pool, you need to develop principles and guidelines that will shape your negotiations on donor recognition.

Anonymity

The issue of donor anonymity deserves a paragraph on its own because it is so often forgotten.

You must respect a donor's desire for anonymity. This is not a matter to be determined by default, assuming that a donor who wants anonymity will take the initiative to say so. Every donor, down to the smallest contributor, must be consulted to determine whether it is permissible to display or reveal the donor's identity in any public arena. To demonstrate that you have received support that cannot be credited by name, the correct form is to end each acknowledgement listing with a phrase such as 'and three anonymous donors'.

How will you keep your donors engaged?

You will employ many different strategies to keep your campaign donors informed and involved: to convey the results and importance of their gifts, enhance their understanding of your work and your mission, draw them into the excitement of the campaign, thank them, create personal relationships, and encourage their loyalty and their continued support. As you design your stewardship plan, there are a few things to keep in mind.

• Personalised attention is crucial. Every donor at every level must be assigned a 'steward'. This means that a specific person on your fundraising staff has clear responsibility for the stewardship of each donor – large donors individually and smaller donors in affiliated groups. The purpose is not only to assure a complete stewardship plan for every donor and group of donors, but also to give each donor a specific, accessible, and responsive contact person within the organisation.

• In earlier chapters we have discussed the role that board members can play in donor stewardship. Wherever possible and appropriate, a trustee or other fundraising volunteer should be actively involved in the stewardship relationship with each of your higher-level donors.

• Trustees also need to be visible to 'lesser' donors. Try to assure the presence of a trustee at events for members and other lower-level donors as the messenger of your gratitude for their support, and as a symbol of their importance to your success.

• Information and communication are also critical elements of stewardship. Only a small proportion of your donors are likely to require formal reports on their grants. But you would do well to report to all your donors periodically on the progress of the campaign and on the progress of your work, illustrating the ways in which their support has furthered your goals. Newsletters are good; so are personalised letters with highlights of the year's accomplishments; so are brief reports on particular aspects of your work that you know are of special interest to certain donors.

• Finally, share the enjoyment. Let your donors participate in the momentum and exhilaration generated by a successful campaign. Your achievements are their achievements too!

CHAPTER NINE

Components of a capital campaign: fundraising strategy

The skills and strategies of fundraising for a capital campaign are, in most ways, the same skills and strategies used in your everyday fundraising activities. But there are some distinctive factors. In the normal course of business you are probably accustomed to a recurring annual cycle, punctuated by the staggered launches and renewals of discrete special projects. A capital campaign requires that you incorporate all your needs over the entire duration of the campaign into an integrated fundraising strategy, and measures incremental progress toward a consolidated financial goal. In this chapter we will consider some important issues in planning fundraising strategy specifically for a capital campaign.

Elements of fundraising strategy

To develop a campaign fundraising strategy, you need to decide when and how you are going to approach each of your prospects, and for what purpose. You can then design appropriate cultivation and stewardship strategies for prospects at different gift levels and with different interests, and create a coordinated timetable and work plan for your staff and fundraising volunteers.

Your first step is to analyse your targets (your goals and your prospects) on four parallel tracks:

- targets organised by timetable
- targets organised by theme
- targets organised by source
- targets organised by sequence.

Unlike many of the exercises in earlier chapters, these four analyses will not fit together in any obvious linear or logical fashion. Rather, they simply give you four different perspectives on the strategic elements you need to consider in making a campaign fundraising plan. You can then assemble these elements in whatever way best serves your needs.

Timetable

In the early planning phase of your campaign, you created a chart of preliminary fundraising goals over the course of the campaign. (See the introduction to Chapter 4.) You can now revisit and refine this chart.

How much money for each of your campaign goals do you need to raise each year? When will the expenses for each stage of your building design and construction have to be paid? When will you need the money to plan and launch each of your new projects and programme initiatives? How does your operating base change from year to year? By answering these queries you can begin to calculate a fundraising goal for each year of the campaign.

This exercise demands that you distinguish between pledges (promises of future payment) and cash. Most campaign gifts of any significant size are likely to be made in the form of multi-year pledges, to be paid out over a specified number of years in specified amounts. Your timetable clarifies your need for ready money, cash in hand to meet the expenses of a given year, and thus helps you determine when pledge payments as well as outright cash gifts need to be received.

Beyond your immediate need for cash, what portion of your campaign goals can be 'front-loaded', that is, raised well before it is scheduled for expenditure? Campaigns that last for more than two or three years can tend to lose a bit of steam as they pass their mid-point. Since many of your largest gifts are likely to be pledged early in the campaign (see the later section entitled *Sequence*), you should project a substantial percentage of the total in the first few years to establish the credibility and create the momentum that will inspire other donors to follow suit. And if endowment is a component of your campaign, remember also that the earlier endowment funds are received, the earlier they begin spinning off revenue that can be used to support operations.

Make a new projection of fundraising goals for each year of the campaign. This is the 'bottom line', the timetable for all fundraising activity on an annual basis right up to the end of the campaign.

Theme

Next, you need to work out which of your prospects is likely to support each of your campaign purposes, and at what level. This again is an extension of an earlier planning exercise, when you assessed the potential of your donor base and prospect pool (see Chapter 4). The charts created in the course of that exercise projected your best guesses for each prospect's gift and area of interest. Now is the time to refine those guesses and integrate them into a fundraising strategy.

This time you will want to organise your campaign purposes thematically, reflecting aspects of your mission and activities that will appeal to the interests of each of your prospects. You can categorise your campaign goals in terms of their subject matter, or the different ways in which they enhance your ability to serve your clients and community, then list prospects under each of these categories. A university, for example, might group prospects by their interest in various academic fields: the sciences, the arts, Asian or American studies, or business. Any one of these thematic categories could bundle together a combination of construction, endowment, project, and operating needs. A cancer charity might be able to identify one group of prospects with a concern for medical research, another concerned with direct services to cancer patients and their families, and yet another concerned with public education about cancer prevention. You will probably also be able to identify a group of prospects who will respond to the broad institutional purposes of your campaign as a whole. These could be excellent sources of unrestricted gifts or gifts that advance several campaign goals at once.

As you see where your prospects fall, you can begin to envisage cultivation and stewardship strategies that will appeal to their interests, suggesting how to tell your story in the most effective way. You can also begin to match up your prospects against your timetable, suggesting where you need to focus your fundraising efforts at any given point in the campaign.

Source

Fundraising strategy is also determined by the nature of your funding sources. The story you tell, the tone of your approach, the kinds of outcomes you project, the opportunities you offer for recognition and acknowledgement will be shaped one way for corporate prospects, another for major gift prospects, and another for members. If a symphony orchestra has identified a large number of corporate prospects for its new hall and for its concert seasons, for example, it might decide to create a mini 'corporate campaign' tailored to the motivations, the language, and the style of the business community. An organisation devoted to preserving local wildlife or a charity working to combat hunger or homelessness might design a special membership campaign focusing on issues that will motivate community-minded citizens to become donors.

Most organisations with a professional development office already segment their fundraising activities by source, and have some staff with specialist knowledge and experience in areas such as major gifts, legacies, membership, corporate sponsorship, and trusts. As you plan the campaign you will probably maintain this segmentation as a way of organising your day-to-day fundraising activity, but you should also examine how this division of labour dovetails with the more thematic approach described in the preceding section. Should you try to meld the two? One way might be to create teams of fundraising specialists that focus on important thematic goals, each member of the team bringing a different type of expertise.

It is entirely a matter of judgement whether you wish to organise your fundraising thematically or by source. Most campaigns end up with a combination of the two; indeed, you may emphasise one or the other at different stages of your campaign. But what is important is that you analyse your timetable, themes, and sources, as outlined here, so that you can examine the different elements that will go into the development of fundraising strategy.

Sequence

Cutting across the three elements just discussed (timetable, theme, and source) is the issue of sequence. The structure of a campaign within a defined period of time with a clear beginning and a clear end requires that you sequence your cultivation of donors in the right order, with a special focus on lead gifts and closing gifts.

Lead gifts, as explained first in Chapter 4, are the largest gifts that occupy the top tiers of your gift table and that collectively account for a substantial proportion (as much as 40% or more) of your campaign revenue. Most lead gifts are made by individuals, but corporations and trusts, and some large government funding sources like the National Lottery, can also be lead donors. Prospects for lead gifts need to be identified in the earliest stages of planning, when you are testing whether your donor base and prospect pool are strong enough to meet your campaign goals. Not all lead gifts necessarily come to fruition at the very beginning of a campaign; in fact, there may be good reason for closing some lead gifts at a later time. (The announcement of a 'blockbuster' lead gift in the third year of a five-year campaign can give new punch to both your fundraising and your public relations.) But it would be dangerous to launch a campaign if you cannot predict where the lead gifts on your gift table will be coming from.

Because lead gifts have such a disproportionate impact on the progress of the campaign, it is essential to sequence the cultivation and negotiation of lead gifts as a discrete issue, separate from and parallel to the development of your other fundraising strategies. Regardless of when these gifts will be closed, begin cultivating and negotiating with your lead gift prospects as early as possible. The feasibility study, discussed in Chapter 5, is the most common starting point for the cultivation of lead gifts. The negotiation of lead gifts can be lengthy and complex. These prospects need to understand where they will fit into the scheme of things and how their gifts will shape the campaign. Donor recognition of lead gifts, especially naming opportunities, must be carefully planned. And because almost all lead gifts are paid out over a period of years, it is important to estimate how pledge payments will fit into your campaign timetable.

Lead gifts are commonly made in support of construction, endowment, and operations in various combinations – the 'big ticket' items in your list of needs where a single large gift can move you well along toward your campaign goals. But a lead gift can also be negotiated for unrestricted support: a gift to the campaign as a whole, to be allocated wherever it is most needed. The fact that a lead gift is unrestricted does not limit options for donor recognition because these options recognise gifts to the campaign in its entirety, not just gifts for a particular purpose. If at all possible, you should try to obtain at least some of your largest gifts in the form of unrestricted campaign support, thus giving you flexibility to achieve all of your campaign goals regardless of the actions of subsequent donors. The more unrestricted support you can negotiate, the more flexibility you will have.

Lead gifts are sometimes fashioned as matching gifts, challenging other donors to match the gift pound for pound. Such 'challenge grants' can be a strong motivation or, if poorly constructed, can become a tremendous obstacle. The key is to shape the challenge to have broad appeal for matching donors, rather than to reflect the narrower perspective of the lead donor.

Board and volunteer leadership will be crucial in assuring that lead gifts are shaped and timed to best meet your needs. It is rare for lead gifts to be cultivated or negotiated without significant trustee involvement.

Sequence is also an issue in planning the gifts to close a campaign. Although it would be delightful to cap your campaign with a spectacular multi-million-pound gift that takes you to the goal line, few campaigns end with a bang. In fact, many campaigns inch toward and across the goal line without much notice (see the next chapter for a discussion of campaign 'phases'), and large gifts that come late in the campaign are sometimes actually allocated toward future, post-campaign fundraising goals.

At the beginning of the campaign, you need to envisage a strategy for ending it. One of the classic strategies is a general public appeal, in effect a 'grassroots' mini-campaign to create a fund that will complete the purposes of the campaign. This serves the dual purpose of reaching your fundraising goal and at the same time giving a wider public, including many people who have never before contributed to your organisation, a sense of ownership in your achievements – and in your future.

Another often-used end strategy is to hold a series of benefit events. Sometimes these are low-key social gatherings, such as picnics or games or drinks parties, at which those attending are asked to contribute to the campaign. Sometimes they are more formal occasions, such as elegant dinners for which tickets are sold at premium prices (covering expenses, with a hefty balance as a contribution to the campaign); these appeal to a more affluent audience, frequently lured by the promise of a well-known name as host or honoured guest. Those who attend benefit events are often attracted more by the prospect of a good time or the social caché than by the mission of the organisation, other than a vague awareness that it is all 'in a good cause'. Some campaigns load their last year with celebratory benefit events of this kind to raise the final cash gifts they need from people who would not otherwise become donors.

As with lead gifts, plan your closing gift strategy early enough in the campaign so that you have set the stage correctly when the moment arrives.

Strategy for operating support

Over and over again throughout this book, it has been emphasised that strengthening your operating base should be your central concern. There is simply no point in opening a splendid new building if you cannot afford to switch on the lights and pay the staff who work within it. Nor can you count a campaign a success if you meet your construction goal to the last pound, but end up with an operating deficit.

You may find it difficult to protect your operating base in the throes of a capital campaign. It is often easier to motivate people to invest in what is new and different than in 'business as usual'. Thus, you must find ways not only to protect but actually to increase your operating base as your capital assets grow in the course of the campaign, and to demonstrate to donors the relationship between operating support and the capacity for growth.

Here are some suggestions for fundraising strategies to protect and expand your operating base in a capital campaign.

• The concept of 'core activities' or 'core costs' is useful as an internal analytical and planning tool (see Chapter 3), but not as a fundraising strategy. In all your communications with prospects and donors, describe the substance of your core activities with as much specificity and clarity as if you were presenting a completely new project. 'We need your support to continue our services this year' is limp compared to 'We must raise £10,000 this year to provide after-school play schemes for 300 children with learning disabilities'.

• Charities are often reluctant to include administrative and overhead costs in their fundraising materials. This is a serious mistake, because it may leave an entire (and often substantial) cost centre under-funded or completely unfunded. You should employ full-cost budgeting in all your applications, whether for operating or project support, including management and administrative salaries, heat, light and rent, insurance, even telephone, photocopying and postage. There are ways to present budgets that fold prorated administration and overhead into line items that describe the substance of your activities. For example, the £10,000 to provide after-school play schemes for 300 children with learning disabilities will incorporate salaries as well as proportionate allocations of the organisation's expenses for heat, light, rent, and other administrative and overhead costs. But even when a funder requires a budget format that shows administration and overhead separately, or is unwilling to support administration and overhead, don't try to hide or understate these costs in an effort to please. It is essential that your donors know your real costs of doing business, even if they are selective in the costs they choose to support.

• A campaign is an opportunity to seek multi-year pledges of operating support from donors who have traditionally supported you on an annual basis. Such pledges give you the assurance of continuity over a period of years, even if the amount of the gift remains the same on an annual basis. Requesting multi-year pledges is a way of demonstrating to your donors the importance of a stable operating base.

• A campaign is an opportunity to persuade donors to increase their operating support by demonstrating how your new capital assets will increase your capacity and your impact, and thus your operating costs.

• You can negotiate with your high- and mid-level donors to incorporate an operating component into every gift, including gifts for construction, endowment, new programme initiatives, and special projects. This technique has been used successfully in many campaigns. Again, it requires that you take the time to explain to your donors the essential link between stability and growth. If they are making a substantial investment in your growth, they can be persuaded to protect that investment by assuring that it rests on a solid foundation of operating support.

Some organisations have an established history of raising operating support through a self-contained annual fund. If you have such a structure and it has worked successfully, there is no reason to change it for a capital campaign. However, the fundraising volunteers and staff who run your annual fund need to develop a strategy for relating the fund to the larger concept and context of the campaign, so that annual fund donors can become an integral part of the effort and an integral factor in its success. And remember that many a major donor has emerged from the ranks of an annual fund. Look to the annual fund as a source of prospects for other campaign needs, incorporating their commitment to operating support into a larger package of campaign goals. Conversely, cultivate your campaign donors as future contributors to the annual fund – an excellent strategy for building the loyalty of new donors to meet your increasing operating costs.

Monitoring your fundraising strategy

Experienced fundraisers know the value of a well-thought-out plan. They also know the value of remaining alert and adaptable to changing circumstances, and of seizing unexpected opportunities as they come along.

Having developed strategies and a work plan to organise the activities of your staff and volunteers, you need also to develop a plan to monitor the results. The pace of activity in a capital campaign does not leave much time for reflection unless you make time. Establish a schedule to review your strategies (see more in Chapter 11), and define criteria for deciding whether, and how well, your strategies are working. The easy answer is they are working if the money is coming in. But look deeper. Here are some questions you might ask as you monitor your progress.

• Are you getting a better response from certain prospect sources than you expected? Possibly your campaign has made you much more visible to the business sector, for example, and corporations are responding more enthusiastically than you had anticipated. Build on success. Think about refining some of your cultivation strategies, developing additional forms of public acknowledgement, recruiting additional fundraising volunteers from the business sector, finding ways to involve corporate employees in the work of your organisation, and reallocating some of your fundraising resources to exploit this unforeseen opportunity.

• Are you not getting the response you had hoped for from certain prospect sources? If some segments of your current donor base are lagging behind your projections, perhaps you have not convinced them that the campaign is creating new assets that will actually improve, not undermine, the work they have so loyally supported in the past. It is not unusual for smaller donors, in particular, to feel that a capital campaign is for 'the rich' and their more modest contributions will just fall into a bottomless pit. How can you correct this perception? On the other hand, despite your best efforts the response from some potentially promising new prospects may have been disappointing. Persistence is a virtue, but dogged persistence in the face of all the evidence is not. Go back to your board and fundraising volunteers to develop new leads; do more prospect research; and ask your campaign donors to open doors for you into a new prospect pool.

• If it appears that you may not be able to reach your annual fundraising goal, what then? Should you simply increase the next year's goal, or add another year on to the campaign? These are not the wisest strategies. Remember that fundraising momentum is likely to be at its highest in the early years of a campaign, so there is probably little to be gained solely by delay. On the assumption that you have followed a careful, systematic process to plan your campaign and identify your funding prospects, it is likely that your problem arises from a single cause: perhaps a catastrophic world event that has diverted philanthropic contributions to other purposes, there has been perhaps a sudden downturn in the economy, or perhaps a hitherto committed donor has failed to come through with an expected lead gift. With this originating cause in mind, go back to an earlier stage in your campaign planning, revisit your donor base and prospect pool and your leadership (see Chapters 4 and 6), and see if you can revise your plan to take account of this unexpected development. You will probably find that your pool of resources is more resilient than you might have realised.

• But perhaps money is coming in faster than you had expected! (It does happen.) One option is simply to declare victory and wind up your campaign early. If you are a small organisation whose campaign is focused solely on constructing a new building, this is usually the best answer. If you are a larger, more complex organisation with multiple goals, a more adventurous option may be to raise your sights: take advantage of the momentum you have created by increasing your goals and extending the length of your campaign. You would have to take this decision with the same meticulous planning you used to launch your original campaign, and you would be opening yourself up to some potential new risks, but it is an option that should be considered. Success often breeds more success.

• As the campaign progresses, your campaign leadership may begin to show signs of burn-out. Check to be sure that you are giving good support to your fundraising volunteers (even those who seem to be most self-reliant) so that their workloads are not becoming too onerous. Don't relax your efforts to recruit new fundraising volunteers, to replace those who may fall away and re-energise those who remain. And make certain that all the work done by your volunteers is warmly appreciated and publicly praised.

• Someone offers you a very large gift for a project that is not in your campaign goals. What should you do? Even if the purpose falls within the spirit of your campaign (and your mission), would a new project divert energy, resources, and attention away from your central goals? What impact would this new project have on your future operating base; has the donor made provision for this, or simply left it as your problem?

Is the donor open to negotiation so that the gift can be shaped to fit your strategic goals? Is this something you really want to do (perhaps, one of the goals defined in your strategic plan that didn't quite make it to the list of top priorities), or are you simply trying to please an important donor? It would not be unusual for a decision of this importance to be made by the board.

This last query illustrates the essential point of planning strategy. Planning gives direction and discipline. But a strategy is just that: a means to an end. Strategies are always open to re-examination and adaptation in order to get the best result under a given set of circumstances. Plan well, and then don't be afraid to let instinct and imagination help carry you toward your goals.

CHAPTER TEN
Staging the campaign

Think of your campaign as a play in four acts, each act staged for a different audience.

The four stages of a capital campaign reflect changes in focus and purpose. Each shapes the way you organise your resources and express your story, and each lays the necessary foundation for the next, building the structure of your campaign in a logical manner from beginning to end. This chapter will review the stages of a capital campaign so that you can anticipate the work you need to do to move from one to the next.

Planning

If you have read this far, you should know a great deal about planning for a capital campaign!

It is in the planning process that you define and justify your priorities, plot your story, identify sufficient resources to support a capital campaign, and develop your fundraising strategy. Every subsequent stage of your campaign should be traceable to the analytical methods and conclusions of your planning process.

The planning stage looks primarily inward. True, your feasibility study requires you to submit your campaign plan, for the first time, to an external, independent assessment. But for the most part, the planning stage is an internal exercise that seeks to uncover relevant facts and make logical judgements based on those facts. It is not a time for wishful thinking, glossing over uncomfortable truths, or flights of rhetoric to impress the outside world. The purpose of planning is not to make a rigid set of rules; the purpose of planning is to explore all contingencies so that you are well prepared for the challenges (both foreseen and unexpected) of a capital campaign.

Do not rush your planning. At several points in earlier chapters you have been advised to consider important questions that might give you reason to stop, re-examine, and take remedial action before moving forward again. Even if you feel pressure to raise money for an urgent need, your chances of success will be much greater if you have planned meticulously. It is often possible to complete the planning stage of a campaign, including a strategic plan, in less than a year, but do not be dismayed if it takes much longer. It will be time well spent.

The 'quiet campaign'

The second stage of the campaign begins with your feasibility study and ends with the public announcement of the campaign. (The feasibility study is structurally part of the planning phase, since the final decision to undertake a campaign is not made until the study is complete. That moment of decision is when the clock on your campaign begins ticking. However, the feasibility study is a significant step in the cultivation of major gift prospects, and is therefore also an essential component of the 'quiet campaign'.)

Despite its name, this stage is anything but quiet. This is the time for you to generate a public image of action, excitement, and 'things going on', and to line up the lead gifts and other major gifts that will move your campaign well forward before it is publicly announced. During the quiet stage, in fact, it will be widely known that your campaign is well under way: word will certainly spread quickly among your active donors and prospects, and most probably among other organisations and charities in your community as well.

These are the principal components of the quiet campaign.

• The feasibility study initiates dialogue with individual members of the board, lead gift and major gift prospects, and important community leaders about the rationale and goals of the campaign, and sets in motion the earliest negotiations for lead gifts.

• The campaign committee and other structures of volunteer fundraising leadership are put in place and begin their work of identifying and cultivating campaign prospects.

• Advance public relations efforts raise the organisation's visibility and pique public interest in preparation for a formal campaign announcement.

• Trustees pledge (or are in negotiation for) their own gifts to the campaign. Remember the importance of the board's financial support for a campaign, both as a sign of commitment and as a precondition of asking others to make gifts (see Chapters 4 and 6).

• Pledges are received for lead gifts. This is called the 'nucleus fund', representing formal pledges of a substantial proportion of the top-tier gifts on your gift table. Most campaigns are not officially launched until a nucleus fund of at least 40–45% or more of the total campaign goal has been assembled.

• Beyond the lead gifts and other major gifts counted toward the nucleus fund, negotiations are well under way for gifts in the middle range of your gift table, so that these donors have an opportunity to be included in the campaign announcement, or are primed to act in the atmosphere of excitement that will follow the campaign announcement.

The quiet stage may last for a third or, in some cases, even half the duration of a capital campaign. By the time you are ready to make a formal campaign announcement, you must be confident that you have enough feasible prospects and enough momentum to achieve your stated campaign goals. Do not feel pressured to launch your campaign officially and publicly until you have completed all the work of this second stage.

Going public

In the third stage of a campaign you are ready to tell your story to the broadest audience you can reach, inviting the public to join with you in an exciting venture.

The official public announcement of a campaign is not really 'news', since your most important prospects already know about the campaign and many have committed their support. Rather, it is more like a formal presentation of your story, couched in optimistic language and imparting the aura of success. The announcement is usually staged as a press event, with your board chair, chief executive, campaign committee chair and other trustees at the head table to explain the goals of the campaign (perhaps with a slide presentation) and to announce your lead gifts. Important community leaders, lead gift donors and major gift prospects will be invited as honoured guests, and everyone will leave with your case statement in hand.

In the quiet campaign you focused intensely on fundraising from the inner circle of lead gift and major gift prospects and your closest, most loyal family of donors, including your trustees. After the campaign announcement you will still pursue opportunities for additional major gifts, of course (and with luck you will have many more of these to your credit as the campaign progresses), but now you need to cast a wider net. The pace of cultivation and stewardship events will pick up markedly. You will look for creative new ways to entice donors at the lower levels of your gift table, and prepare to implement your plan for the closing gifts of the campaign. This is the time for a serious re-examination of your fundraising strategy to make certain that you are targeting your resources in the most productive manner. It is also the time to address any warning signs that you might be lagging in progress toward one or more of your campaign goals, and to adjust your strategy accordingly.

Closing the campaign

Oddly enough, it is not always obvious when a campaign ends. You may reach all of your fundraising goals at the predetermined closing date of the campaign, with your new building about to open and operating support secure at its projected higher level; in this case, it is clear that the campaign is over. But most campaigns are not quite so neat.

Many campaigns just seem to keep going, in the sense that fundraising does not slow down when the appointed date and goal are reached. New projects and new needs are on the table, your current donors seem ready to give again, promising new prospects have been cultivated, and the momentum has not abated. In fact, as we noted in the last chapter, your momentum may be so strong that you actually decide to increase your campaign goals and keep going for another year or so. But at some point, it is important to announce closure. One reason is to confirm the public perception of a successful organisation that has the ability to achieve its stated goals. Another is to thank your donors and your leadership for their accomplishments, and let them savour the pleasure of a job well done.

Most campaigns celebrate their completion with thank-you receptions or other events for their donors. The end of the campaign is publicised in the press, announcing the amount of money raised and describing the results – a building ready to open, endowment funds in the bank, or a flourishing new programme serving the community. A final campaign report, often in the form of a newsletter, is published and sent to donors. (Note that organisations that have surpassed their fundraising goals may decide not to include all gifts in the campaign total. Some large gifts received late in the campaign, or gifts for new needs and projects that were not in the original campaign plan, may be held over for announcement at a later time.)

You are now out of 'campaign mode'. However, your work has not ended, as we will see in the final chapter of this book. But first, we will take a brief look at the structures and procedures you will need to manage a capital campaign.

CHAPTER ELEVEN

Managing the campaign

Running a capital campaign will inevitably strain your management capacity. After all, you already have your hands full running the existing programmes and services that constitute your raison d'être, and raising the money to support them. Even if you take on extra staff for the duration, a great many people in the organisation will have to assume added responsibilities related to the campaign effort, and nearly everyone's job will be affected by the intensity and stress of campaign fundraising.

This chapter will suggest structures and procedures that can help you manage the campaign in a rational, orderly fashion. Behind these procedures lies a crucial principle: that the campaign must be managed in a way that incorporates its goals and methods into the work of the organisation as a whole. The campaign is not a separate entity: it is simply the umbrella for all your fundraising activities over a specified period of time. A campaign that drifts into its own parallel universe is likely to stray off course, breed disaffection and disruption, and ultimately lose the united organisational commitment it needs to succeed.

Campaign oversight and coordination

Once your board has authorised the launch of a capital campaign, you must develop a mechanism to oversee its management on an ongoing basis. The usual mechanism is a campaign steering committee, a coordinating body representing all major staff departments that have campaign responsibilities. These include at least:

- the office of the chief executive
- the development (fundraising) department
- the finance (budget and accounting) department
- the public relations and marketing department
- those departments or programmes directly involved in designing and implementing the new capital assets created by the campaign.

The list is not definitive; add any other departments or staff positions that will play a continuing role in your campaign. It is customary to appoint department heads to the campaign steering committee; however, in some instances it may be more appropriate or feasible to deputise a second-in-command or other senior staff member. Because the committee's brief is oversight and coordination, it requires continuity, and for this reason you would do well to appoint more than one staff representative from each principal participating department.

The campaign steering committee will meet regularly, possibly every two or three weeks in the early phases of the campaign, monthly or less frequently in periods of less intense activity. The procedures of the steering committee will be different in a large organisation (where departments and staff are widely dispersed) from a smaller, more compact organisation where staff are in virtually daily contact. In a large organisation, for example, it may be useful to appoint a sub-committee to maintain coordination and move the work of the steering committee forward between meetings. Otherwise, you may simply want to designate one or two committee members to keep and distribute minutes and prepare meeting agendas.

Design your campaign steering committee to suit your own structure and working style. However it is constituted, its duties encompass at least the following areas.

• Review of fundraising revenue. This means cumulative progress reports on gifts and pledges received toward each of the campaign goals, and even more critically, reviews of cash gifts and pledge payments received toward the fundraising goals established for each financial year, especially goals for operating support. Any early warning signs need to be spotted, analysed for their cause, and addressed quickly with remedial action.

• Overall financial status. Recall (Chapter 3) that your total financial needs presuppose income other than fundraising revenue, including earned income and statutory funding and contracts. Any fluctuations, up or down, in these sources, as well as fluctuations in projected expenses, could affect your campaign goals. The campaign must be monitored within the context of the organisation's overall financial position.

• Analysis of lead gifts and other major gifts received, pending or in negotiation. Because these gifts represent such a substantial proportion of your fundraising goal, it is essential that everyone understand the terms and timing of each large gift, its likely impact on the projects and programmes for which it is intended, and the implications of any naming opportunities or other stewardship benefits attached to the gift.

• Campaign activities that require close inter-departmental coordination. These might include preparation of the case statement and campaign announcement, major cultivation and stewardship events, the content of campaign publicity, and celebrations to open a building or launch a new programme.

• Reports of significant changes in the scope of ongoing operations and projects, including budgets. No organisation is static, and over the course of the campaign it is natural to expect some changes in substance, personnel, and costs. Construction projects and major new programme initiatives are of special concern, as these frequently change markedly between their initial plans and their completion. Everyone who communicates with donors and prospects needs to know that they are accurately representing the organisation's work.

• Review of current campaign leadership activity. Chapter 6 described the fundraising mandate of the campaign committee and the responsibilities of all staff to support the campaign's fundraising volunteers in their cultivation and stewardship activities. All departments must be aware of their obligations to these volunteers, and ready to be called upon as needed.

Communication and the sharing of information are among the most powerful tools of management. The campaign steering committee is a vehicle for maintaining horizontal, inter-departmental communication – and thereby, inter-departmental coordination. But it can also foster two-way vertical communication of information within departments. The members of the steering committee are responsible for disseminating within their own departments all pertinent information, discussion, and decisions from the meetings of the steering committee, and for bringing to the committee information, questions, and concerns that arise within their departments.

A final word about the campaign steering committee's 'powers'. The mandate of the steering committee is oversight and coordination, not policy. If issues of policy do arise (for example, the possibility of a substantial change in the campaign plan or goals, a major shift in fundraising strategy, or questions about a potentially controversial gift) these need to be referred to the board or chief executive or other authority in accordance with your structure and rules of governance.

Financial information management

A subset of campaign management issues concerns finances. A capital campaign will not only impose a heavier workload on your budget and accounting departments, but also require detailed procedures for tracking and reporting revenue and expenditures (see Chapter 4).

You will need to assure the capacity to 'follow the money': to allocate every campaign gift to the correct purposes and track its expenditure against clearly defined budgets. This is not the place to discuss specific accounting and budgeting methods; see the *Further Reading* section at the end of this book for more on these subjects. But as you consider the management of financial information in a capital campaign, remember that you will be called upon to report to your board, to the campaign steering committee, and to your donors the receipt and expenditure of gifts on three levels: in the aggregate, by goal and purpose, and gift-by-gift. Your budget and accounting staff will also lead the work of developing a timetable of cash gifts and pledge payments needed for each financial year based on budget projections for expenditure, and of monitoring and reporting progress toward these goals (see Chapter 9).

One device that has proved useful in many campaigns is the appointment of a small inter-departmental working group to analyse all restricted gifts. (One such group was dubbed RATS: the Revenue Analysis and Tracking Squad.) It consists of staff appointed from development, budget, and accounting, and meets on a regular (perhaps monthly) basis to review the terms and conditions for every restricted gift, to allocate each gift or the specified portion of each gift to the correct fund in the organisation's accounts against the correct budget lines, and to describe and calendar any required financial reports to the donor. Representatives of appropriate programme departments or projects are invited to participate as necessary to discuss gifts in support of their activities. This is another important level of inter-departmental communication and coordination.

Board oversight and evaluation

The board is the final authority for the oversight of a capital campaign. Based on its responsibilities of governance (to establish overall organisational policy, to preserve organisational integrity, and to ensure adequate organisational resources) the board is the ultimate monitor of campaign progress and arbiter of campaign strategy.

The board, of course, has already played a leading role in the campaign: in guiding strategic planning and approving the final strategic plan, and in guiding campaign planning and authorising the launch of the capital campaign. It is linked to the campaign on an ongoing basis through its representation on the campaign committee, and its members have participated individually as donors.

Every meeting of the board should include a campaign report, presented by the chair or the chief executive or the chair of the campaign committee, or all three acting in tandem. The report should cover progress toward the total and component campaign goals, announcement of lead gifts and other significant gifts and grants (confidentially, if these gifts are not yet appropriate to reveal publicly), and progress on the implementation of campaign projects. And a few other topics deserve notice: the credit due to trustees and other fundraising volunteers in obtaining important gifts; the participation of trustees in cultivation and stewardship events; and the board's own financial contribution. (The latter should not be attributed to named board members unless they wish to be identified, but the board should monitor its own record in terms of the percentage of trustees contributing and the aggregate amount of its gifts.) If you have an executive committee or other sub-committee of the board that has governing authority between board meetings, it too should receive regular reports on campaign progress.

It is natural to wish to draw the most optimistic picture, and also to encourage the board's enthusiasm by emphasising the positive. But do not forget that the board has serious responsibilities of governance. If potential problems are brewing (a lag in operating support, unexpected delays or cost overruns in a building project, for example) the board needs to be forewarned if these might jeopardise the organisation's well-being or develop into real obstacles to campaign success. There are ways to present these issues as problems with solutions, and to invoke the board's help in implementing those solutions.

As you approach the end of the campaign the board needs to evaluate the ways in which the organisation has been changed by the campaign itself and by the new assets it has acquired through the campaign, and begin charting your future. This will be the subject of the final chapter of this book.

CHAPTER TWELVE

After the campaign: what next?

You would not have started a capital campaign if you had not wanted change. But it is always difficult to predict all the many and varied manifestations of change, and even more difficult to absorb them into your structure and organisational culture and day-to-day activities.

The key to managing change is to plan for it. Though it sounds contradictory, you can even plan for unforeseen change. The planning mechanisms described in this book can continue to serve you well even after the campaign is over. In this chapter we will look at some of the ways in which a capital campaign generates change, and how you can harness change to your advantage.

How a capital campaign will change you

The most obvious result of a capital campaign is growth. You now have more assets to manage, and more assets to support. That is a challenge. But you also have more assets on which to build new programmes and services, expand your reach, and move a few steps closer to your vision of a successful organisation and a healthy community. That is also a challenge. Thus, you need to develop the capacity to manage a larger organisation, but you also have a stronger foundation for creativity, and for taking risks.

The campaign has honed critical organisational skills. In some areas this is apparent: in fundraising, public relations, and financial management, among others. But it can also be found in unexpected places. For example, through their participation in campaign planning and fundraising, the staff who serve your homeless clients or preserve rare objects in your museum collections can become visible and articulate advocates for your organisational mission, and learn how to communicate the impact and importance of their own jobs with clarity and passion. All these skills strengthen your capacity for fundraising and community relations in the future.

You have probably become more professional in your skills and standards of performance, in your management structure and procedures, and in your organisational culture. Despite the obvious advantages, this is sometimes a cause for lament. Many charities begin with a small group of inspired, dedicated people and function brilliantly for years in an atmosphere of intimacy and informality. There is no question that the demands of a capital campaign, and the growth that it engenders, can undermine that atmosphere. There may be resentments and friction, even some defections, if the process of professionalisation is perceived as a kind of 'culture clash'.

The campaign will both strengthen and test your board's capacity for leadership. Through their participation in the campaign, trustees have deepened their commitment and sharpened their own skills and confidence. But the campaign has probably also left some of them feeling burned out, impatient to turn their attention elsewhere, and it has almost certainly demonstrated the need for continuing board development.

The campaign has raised your public profile. More people are now aware of who you are, what you do, and how you do it. This is fertile ground for future growth. You have an opportunity to attract more donors, more volunteers, more press attention, more clients, and wider audiences. But the spotlight will fade quickly if you do not grasp the opportunity quickly and vigorously.

The time and care you expended on the planning and preparations for a capital campaign should have demonstrated the importance of defining your organisational future in an orderly, systematic manner. More specifically, it should have demonstrated that fundraising is most productive when it is embedded securely in a strategic context, directed toward a clearly articulated mission, and targeted to clearly established goals and agreed priorities.

You can prepare for change if you know what to look for, and you can make change into a positive force instead of a disruption if you have a rational process for shaping your responses. If you have followed the strategic planning and campaign planning structures outlined in this book, you will know the essential elements of a good planning process. As you go forward, keep in mind these principles:

Key principles of good planning

• Planning is most effective when it is designed as a consultative process involving the greatest possible number of participants. No opinion is irrelevant; no staff position is too 'junior' to be included in the debate. Remember that when people have been consulted and feel that their expertise has been respected and their advice seriously considered, they are more likely to remain motivated and committed, even if their point of view has not prevailed.

• Planning is most effective when it is a continuing process rather than an episodic event. We have seen how strategic planning moves naturally into campaign planning, and how conscientious monitoring of the campaign plan can lead to the reconsideration of strategy. As the end of the campaign approaches, it is time to continue the planning process to define the organisation's future.

How to build on your achievements

It is easy to understand why, at the end of a campaign, you would look forward to a period of relative calm and the chance to slow down for a while. But there is a critical period following a capital campaign when it is imperative to exploit the assets and momentum you have created before unique opportunities are lost. This does not mean that you have to maintain the high intensity of 'campaign mode', but it does mean that you have to continue moving forward.

It is time to return to planning.

Your strategic plan set the framework for your capital campaign, or, read in reverse, your capital campaign was one of the strategies you chose to achieve the highest-priority organisational goals identified in your strategic plan. If you have followed the process described in Chapter 2, you have revisited the plan periodically, making any necessary adjustments (for example, in response to significant but unforeseen changes in the external environment), and monitoring progress toward your strategic goals.

By the last year of the campaign, when the finish line is in sight, you need to conceive a post-campaign future. If you re-read your strategic plan, you will find that the general outlines of that future are already drawn: in your mission, your values, and your vision statement. You will need to define a new set of challenges and opportunities in light of the accomplishments of your campaign, and from them, a new set of short-term goals. But you will probably find that the general direction of your strategic plan has not changed dramatically. You have simply moved farther along the road toward the realisation of your vision.

Before the campaign ends, your board should prepare to start a new strategic planning process. Since you laid the groundwork with your first strategic plan, this time you may find that the process moves more smoothly, but do not be tempted to rush or cut corners. There is no need to have a new strategic plan in hand when the campaign ends, only the need to be engaged in the process itself. In fact, it would be wiser not to adopt a new strategic plan until the implications of the changes brought about by your capital campaign are clear.

You also need to evaluate the board's capacity to lead a changed organisation. The campaign may well have brought some 'stars' to the forefront and attracted a number of new volunteers and major donors who might be good candidates for board membership. It should certainly have confirmed the importance of board financial support and participation in fundraising. But it may also have exhausted some trustees, who are now ready to move on, and highlighted areas for new trustee recruitment. Look again at the board assessment methods described in Chapter 4, and begin to define your targets for future board development. If this assessment goes hand in hand with a renewed strategic planning process, you should be able to see clearly the kinds of trustee attributes and skills you will need to lead the organisation in the future.

Finally, the success of the campaign is a tribute to your fundraising expertise – and to the compelling power of your mission. Past donors have demonstrated their faith in you by increasing their support; you have brought important new donors into your circle; and you are now visible to an even wider field of prospects who may become donors in the future. Don't relax your fundraising efforts. You need to secure a higher operating base to support your new assets, and ahead lies the expectation of more programme expansion and new initiatives. Continue your stewardship of current donors; and develop interesting ways to cultivate new prospects. Your success can be sustained if you build wisely on the accomplishments of your capital campaign.

Appendix
Further Reading

All of the publications listed below are available from the Directory of Social Change.

Voluntary Sector Planning and Management

The Complete Guide to Business and Strategic Planning for Voluntary Organisations
Alan Lawrie
DSC
2001

Fundraising Management: Analysis, Planning and Practice
Adrian Sargeant & Elaine Jay
Routledge
2004

The Charity Trustee's Handbook
Mike Eastwood
DSC
2001

Boards That Work
David Fishel
DSC
2003

Fundraising Skills

Fundraising from Grant-Making Trusts and Foundations
Karen Gilchrist & Margo Horsley
DSC/CAF
2000

Corporate Fundraising
Valerie Morton, editor
DSC/CAF/ICFM
2nd edition, 2002

Why Rich People Give
Theresa Lloyd
Association of Charitable Foundations
2004

Organising Special Events for Fundraising and Campaigning
John F Gray & Stephen Elsden
DSC/CAF
2000

Looking After Your Donors
Karen Gilchrist
DSC/CAF
2000

Sources of Funding

Find the Funds: A New Approach to Fundraising Research
Christopher Carnie
DSC/CAF
2000

A Guide to the Major Trusts 2005/2006, 2 volumes
Tom Traynor
DSC
7th edition, 2005
Volume 1 covers the top 400 UK trusts giving individually in the region of £300,000 to £650 million each year; Volume 2 covers the next 1,500 UK trusts, giving individually in the region of £30,000 to £300,000 each year.

DSC also publishes guides to local trusts in Greater London, the Midlands, the North of England, the South of England, Wales and Scotland.

The Guide to UK Company Giving
John Smyth
DSC
5th edition, 2005

Fundraising from Europe
Christopher Carnie
Chapel & York
2003

A Guide to European Union Funding: Accessing Europe's Largest Donor
ECAS
11th edition, 2005

See also three DSC databases with up-to-date information on trust, company, and government funding sources: www.trustfunding.org.uk (by subscription) www.companygiving.org.uk (by subscription) www.government funding.org.uk (free)

About the Directory of Social Change

DSC is the leading provider of information and training for the voluntary sector. It publishes an extensive range of guides, handbooks, and CD-ROMs, covering subjects such as fundraising, management, communication, finance and law. DSC has a range of subscription-based websites containing a wealth of information on funding from trusts and companies. DSC runs more than 350 courses each year. These take place throughout England and Scotland and cover topics such as: fundraising; management; personnel and training; personal development; communication; finance; and law. DSC conferences, many of which run on an annual basis, include the Charity Management Conference, the Charity Accountants' Conference, and the Charity Law Conference.

For details of all our activities, and to order publications and book courses, go to www.dsc.org.uk, call 08450 777707 or e-mail publications@dsc.org.uk

The Directory of Social Change

24 Stephenson Way
London
NW1 2DP

Federation House
Hope Street
Liverpool
L1 9BW

Other Publications from the Directory of Social Change

All the following fundraising titles are published by DSC, unless otherwise stated, and are available from:

DSC Books
Directory of Social Change
24 Stephenson Way
London
NW1 2DP

Call 08450 777707 or e-mail publications@dsc.org.uk for more details and for a free publications catalogue. You can also view and order online at the DSC website (www.dsc.org.uk).

The fundraising series

Published in association with CAF and the Institute of Fundraising.

Community Fundraising
Edited by Harry Brown

Volunteer networks are a key resource for fundraising, but are often not appreciated as they should be. This new title demonstrates how to make the most of your volunteers. It covers:

- what community fundraising is
- why people volunteer, the value of volunteers and staff attitudes to volunteers
- the recruitment, retention and development of volunteers
- the management of staff working with volunteers
- case studies from a range of different types of charities – and what can be learned from these.

192 pages, 1st edition, 2002 ISBN 1 900360 98 5

Corporate Fundraising
Edited by Valerie Morton

Corporate Fundraising is a fast-moving area and the second edition of this book has been completely revised and updated to include:

- new chapters on corporate social responsibility and on evaluation
- a new appendix on the internet
- a revised section on the legal and tax framework
- a range of new case studies from major charities and companies such as NCH, Diabetes UK, One2One and the Mencap–Transco partnership.

The book continues to offer a comprehensive overview, detailing the variety of ways in which charities and companies may work together to mutual advantage, and addressing key issues around ethics and standards.

200 pages, 2nd edition, 2002 ISBN 1 903991 00 5

Fundraising Databases
Peter Flory

Computerised databases are an essential tool for fundraising, but fundraisers often lack the technical background to help them choose a suitable database and use it effectively. This new book provides a clear framework for making and implementing such decisions. It explains what a database is and how it works, before going on to examine:

- why fundraisers need a database
- the functions of a fundraising database
- future trends

Case studies from a range of charities are used throughout to illustrate the points made.

160 pages, 1st edition, 2001 ISBN 1 900360 91 8

Fundraising Strategy
Redmond Mullin

The key to successful fundraising is rigorous strategic planning and this influential title has become essential reading for all serious fundraisers, as a background to the whole series. The second edition draws on some more recent examples, such as the NSPCC Full Stop campaign, to further clarify the principles and process of strategy and demonstrate its place in fundraising campaigns. The book:

- discusses the concept of strategy and its relevance to not-for-profit bodies
- outlines the planning process for designing and implementing the strategy
- provides case studies of different strategies in different types and sizes of funding programmes
- has been fully updated to take into account important changes in areas such as the tax regime and the National Lottery.

160 pages, 2nd edition, 2002 ISBN 1 903991 22 6

Legacy Fundraising
The Art of Seeking Bequests
Edited by Sebastian Wilberforce

This unique guide to one of the most important sources of revenue for charities has been revised and updated to include new material on telephone fundraising, forecasting income, and profiling. It also contains the full text of the new Institute of Fundraising Code of Practice on legacy fundraising. Contributions from a range of experts in the field cover both strategy and techniques, and are complemented by perspectives from donors and their families. The breadth of coverage and accessible style ensure that, whether you are an established legacy fundraiser or new to the field, this book is a must.

224 pages, 2nd edition, 2001 ISBN 1 900360 93 4

Trust Fundraising
Edited by Anthony Clay

This book outlines a variety of approaches to trusts that will save trustees' time and ensure greater success for fundraising by:

- emphasising the importance of research and maintaining records
- demonstrating the value of using contacts and a personal approach
- reinforcing the need for detailed planning of a strategy
- showing how to make an approach to trusts, and how not to
- stressing the importance of continued contact with a trust.

152 pages, 1st edition, 1999 ISBN 1 85934 069 5

Other fundraising titles from DSC

General

Effective Fundraising
Luke FitzHerbert, 1st edition, 2004

The Complete Membership Handbook – A guide to managing friends, members and supporters schemes
Liz Hill and Brian Whitehead, 1st edition, 2004, published in association with Arts Professional

Writing Better Fundraising Applications
Michael Norton and Mike Eastwood, 3rd edition, 2002, published in association with the Institution of Fundraising

The Complete Fundraising Handbook
Nina Botting and Michael Norton, 4th edition, 2001, published in association with the Institution of Fundraising

Trusts

A Guide to Major Trusts Volume 1 2005/2006 – The Top 400 Trusts
Tom Traynor and Alan French

A Guide to Major Trusts Volume 2 2005/2006 – A Further 1,200 Trusts
Dave Griffiths, Chris McGuire and Rebecca Ryland

Directory of Grant-making Trusts 2005/2006
DSC, published in association with CAF

The Grant-making Trusts CD-ROM
This annually updated resource is packed with information about more than 4,500 UK grant-making trusts giving over £3.1 billion a year. 5th edition, 2005, published in association with CAF, with software development by FunderFinder

www.trustfunding.org.uk
This subscription-based website contains all the same data as the Grant-making Trusts CD-ROM, but is regularly updated throughout the year. Subscribers will be sent e-mails alerting them when updates are made. Subscriptions run for 12 months from the date you subscribe

For individuals

The Educational Grants Directory 2004/2005
Alan French, Dave Griffiths, Emma Jepson, Chris McGuire and Rebecca Ryland

A Guide to Grants for Individuals in Need 2004/2005
Alan French, Dave Griffiths, Emma Jepson and Rebecca Ryland, £29.95

www.grantsforindividuals.org.uk
This subscription-based website contains the same data as *The Guide for Individuals in Need* and *The Educational Grants Directory* and is updated regularly throughout the year. Subscribers are sent e-mails alerting them when updates are made

Companies

The Guide to UK Company Giving
John Smyth, 5th edition, 2005
Includes details of over 500 companies in the UK that give a combined total of £290 million in cash donations to voluntary and community organisations. It includes 60 companies never before listed in this guide

Further sources of help and information 227
The CD-ROM Company Giving Guide
All the information in *The Guide to UK Company Giving* is available on this searchable CD-ROM.
4th edition, 2005, with software development by FunderFinder

www.companygiving.org.uk
This subscription-based website contains the same data as *The CD-ROM Company Giving Guide* but it is regularly updated throughout the year. Relevant tailor-made updates are sent to subscribers when new additions are made

Finding Company Sponsors for Good Causes
Chris Wells, 1st edition, 2000

Government

www.governmentfunding.org.uk
This website developed in partnership with the Active Communities Unit of the Home Office currently covers grants available from four contributing government departments

European Union

A Guide to European Union and other Funding for NGOs – Accessing Europe's Largest Donor
Published by European Citizen Action Service (ECAS), 11th edition, 2004

Specialist funding guides

The Arts Funding Guide
Susan Forrester and David Lloyd, 6th edition, 2002

The Environmental Funding Guide
Susan Forrester and Dave Casson, 3rd edition, 1998

The Schools Funding Guide
Nicola Eastwood, Anne Mountfield and Louise Walker, 1st edition, 2001

The Sports Funding Guide
Nicola Eastwood, 2nd edition, 1999, published in association with Sport England

The Youth Funding Guide
Nicola Eastwood, 2nd edition, 2002

Index